T0209104

THE BLACK ART OF WAR

Hannibal's 99 Truths

JAMES W. PETERSON III

authorHOUSE®

AuthorHouse™
1663 Liberty Drive
Bloomington, IN 47403
www.authorhouse.com
Phone: 1 (800) 839-8640

Published by AuthorHouse   05/18/2020

ISBN: 978-1-7283-3934-4 (sc)
ISBN: 978-1-7283-3933-7 (e)

"Do I want to see you eaten by vultures and hyenas after the next battle, merely because you were too stupid or lazy to understand that what I am trying to teach you today will save you tomorrow?"

-Zulu General Mgobozi Msane to new Zulu recruits, 1818

* * * * *

"Armed with the knowledge of our past, we can with confidence charter a course for our future."

-Malcolm X

Dedication

To the Avery Family• The Peterson family• And the Singleton family

Acknowledgements

A special thank you to Regina Singleton & Princess Singleton for their invaluable contributions to this project.

Contents

Introduction To Book

"Men are never as helpless, nor as clever as they

Believe themselves to be."

--Truth LXXXII

Africa's greatest warrior speaks his mind!

Praised as one of history's greatest strategists, Hannibal Barca (247-183BC) is best known---and in his own time was much respected **and feared!**----*for* his daring battlefield strategies, not the least of which was his "impossible" crossing of the "impassible" mountains of the southern European Alps with over 40,000 African warriors and war-elephants, attacking and defeating his life-long enemy the Romans again and again at their own game on their own home-court!

Both Hannibal's courage and cunning have since been studied by all the masterful men and women worldwide who've come after him, his ingenuity and exploits when fearlessly facing off against the "all-mighty" Roman Empire providing the guidebook for slave revolts and rebellions against oppressive authority down through history, from Spartacus to Nat Turner, while also serving as the inspiration for African resistance movements like the 20th century Kenyan *Mau-Mau* and for African-American social movements like The Black Panthers.

It's no secret how Hannibal's legendary battle tactics helped inspire the conquests of other equally-legendary African leaders who followed in his footsteps, from Egypt's Baibars ei-Rukn down to the great Shaka Zulu.

Indeed, Hannibal's savvy strategies and tactics helped craft many a winning strategy throughout history, down to the lightning swift and effective campaigns of 21ˢᵗ century African-American strategists like *Desert Storm* hero General Colin Powell.

Off the battlefield, Hannibal's equally masterful skill at negotiation, his craft and cunning, became required reading for master manipulators like the wily Queen Cleopatra, as well as for the movers and shakers of our own era.

Still today we and see his savvy strategies mirrored and hear winning wisdom echoed in the triumphs of Civil Rights icons and religious leaders, African-American politicians, as well as in the successes of celebrities and entrepreneurs, from Donald Trump to Russell Simmons.

That's because, for us today, Hannibal's hard-won life lessons-his *99 Truths*- still ring true, *truths* we can use to help guide us to personal awareness and achievement-on the battlefield, in the boardroom, even in the bedroom!

And if Hannibal's 99 jewels of wisdom could be summed up, it would be in the simple concept that *endeavor must exceed environment*:

> "Test yourself with fire and ice, sand and sea, bile and blood, before your enemies do."   ---Truth LXXII

In other words, you have to be stronger than your street!

In their *MIND WARRIOR: STRATEGIES FOR TOTAL MENTAL*

Domination[1] authors Haha Lung and Chris Prowant assure us that no other single man was more responsible for building the Roman Empire----than Rome's greatest enemy Hannibal.

Lung and Prowant also refer to Hannibal as "The Sun Tzu of the West," thus comparing him to the 5ᵗʰ century Chinese martial arts master who wrote the original *Art of War* (called *Ping-fa* in Chinese).

---

[1] Citadel Press, 2010:154

Yes, that is Hannibal we hear laughing from beyond the grave since this praise echoes Truths II and VI of his "99 Truths" where he, somewhat sarcastically, gives "thanks" to his enemies-Rome and others- for *challenging* him, for making him make himself stronger.

Hannibal's times were not our times.

Yet like men faced with challenge in all lands and in all times, Hannibal faced many of the same physical and psychological challenges people in general and young warriors in particular face:

* Challenges to their strength and endurance,

* Challenging questions of honor and duty and responsibility to friends and family.

* And, yes, even settling scores with enemies-either through peaceful negotiation, else by overwhelming them with unexpected strategy!

Thus the same tricks, techniques, and tactics Hannibal the Conqueror used to confuse, cower, and ultimately conquer his enemies on the bloody battlefield are the same kinds of successful plans and ploys and projects other men and women have used down through the centuries to conquer and control in politics, in business, in love.

As Hannibal points out in his Truth VI, a "good" enemy makes us get out of bed in the morning, gives us a reason to work out, to sweat, to "just do it!"

It doesn't matter in today's world if you call your particular enemy a "challenger", "competition", "rival", or even "opportunity", you still have to get up off the couch, put on your sweats, and purposely prepare yourself for "doing battle"... or else, sure as the sun comes up in the morning, you'll lose out and your "challenger" will get in the first punch, your "competition" will make the sale before you do, your "rival" will win the love of your life away from you.

And "opportunity" will walk away before you ever even hear it knocking at your door. Sometimes-oft times-we end up being our own worst enemy. Or, worse yet, we don't realize who our *true* enemies really are:

* The abusive spouse or other family member who's constantly putting us down; undermining our feelings of self-worth, preventing us from getting a better job, from going to back to school, preventing us from taking that vocational course or self-improvement class.

* Those friends always warning us of all the bad that can happen to us unless we act like and dress like and think like everybody else.

* And that so-called "friend" who's all-too-quick to shove a loaded gun into our angry hand....

In his time, Hannibal too wrestled with these same sorts of problems, with these same kinds of nay-sayers (Truth LXXII), fair-weather friends (Truth LXX), and back-stabbers (Truth LXX).

And still he conquered.

Now it's our turn!

* * * * *

"Why your grandfather was Nat Turner; your grandfather was Toussaint L'Ouverture; your grandfather was Hannibal. It was your grandfather's hands who forged civilization and it was your grandmother's hands who rocked the cradle of civilization."   ---Malcolm X[2]

---

[2] *'By Any Means Necessary, Pathfinder, 1970*

The Life & Times of Hannibal the Conqueror

Three hundred years before Jesus walked the earth, 800 years before Muhammad first took up the sword, in the third century BC, the city-nation of Rome was already well on its way to becoming the most powerful force in Europe.

After conquering all of Italy and much of the surrounding territories in Europe, the Roman Empire would eventually come to rule over all the lands around the Mediterranean Sea, including the Middle East, Egypt, and much of North Africa.

Back then, the only "competitor" preventing the Romans from extending their control deeper into Africa was the great North African city-nation of Carthage, whose own "empire" covered what is now the modem nations of Tunisia, Libya, Algeria, and a fair piece of the island of Sicily.

Carthage also controlled what are now the European countries of Spain and Portugal, back then called *Hispania and Lusitania.*

As the wealth and power of Carthage grew, Rome became both paranoid and jealous of how Carthage's great ships were trading goods from one end of the Mediterranean to the other: from Egypt to Spain, as far north in the Atlantic Ocean as the British Isles, and south down the west coast of Africa.

Fearless Carthage captains even sailed west from Africa to discover and trade in the lands found there. This was two thousand years before Christopher Columbus would make a similar trip! There is even evidence Cartage traded with the very first "African Americans", the ancient Black *Olmec* empire of central America.

Why Didn't Somebody Tell Me?

The African "Folsom People" lived in what is now the southwest United States I 0 to 15 *thousand* years ago before Columbus arrived in "The New World".[3]

It was inevitable these two heavyweights, Rome and Carthage, would square off against one another, with the whole of the Mediterranean Sea as their boxing ring.

In the 2nd and 3'd centuries BC, Rome and Carthage went to war with one another three times, in what the Romans called "The *Punic* Wars".

During the First Punic War (264-241 BC) Hannibal's father Hamilcar Barca was leader of Carthage's armed forces. During the Second Punic War (218-201 BC) Hannibal was in command, with his three brothers Hasdrubal, Hanno, and Mago serving under him.

*   *   *   *   *

The people of Carthage called themselves *"Sidonians"* and *"Ttrians"* but the Greeks referred to them as *"Phonecians "*, meaning "dark-skinned."[4]

In the Latin language of the Romans "Phonecian" became *"Peoni"*, *then "Punic"*.

The "Phonecians" originally came from the cities of Sidon and Tyre along the coast of the Middle East, what is now Lebanon and northern Israel.

---

[3] Anderson, 1997: 65
[4] DeBeer, 1969

The best sailors of their time, these Phonecians traded with all the peoples in all lands around the Mediterranean Sea: from the Pharaohs of Egypt in the east, to the Celtic "barbarians" of Spain in the west, eventually establishing the rich and powerful trading colony of Carthage in North Africa.

When their hometowns of Sidon and Tyre in the Middle East were overrun by Assyrian invaders, Carthage became an independent city and began establishing trading colonies of its own in Spain and, most importantly, on Sicily, the large island strategically-situated between Italy and North Africa.

*   *   *   *   *

Jealous over Carthage's growing prosperity and influence to begin with, Rome used Carthage's "intrusion" into Sicily as the excuse to start the First Punic War, which was fought mostly on the island of Sicily and in the waters around it, with Hamilcar Baca in overall command of Carthage forces.

For some time, Carthage had the upper hand in this war since they possessed superior-fearsome! --warships that could easily overtake and overpower the smaller, slower Roman warships. More importantly they could easily sink Roman troop transports carrying Legiounaires from Italy to fight on Sicily.

Whenever possible, the wily Harnilcar avoided directly fighting the formidable Roman Legions head-to-head on land, where Rome was near unbeatable. As a result, a stalemate soon arose with Rome controlling the land and Carthage ruling the sea.

The tide literally turned against Carthage however when one of her warships accidentally ran aground and was captured by the Romans who then took the ship apart to see how it was built.

"Reverse-engineering" the captured vessel, the Romans were soon building warships as strong and as fast as their enemy's, adding a special gang-plank that could hook onto Carthage ships and create a bridge across which Roman Legionnaires could march from one ship to the other, easily capturing Carthage's ships.

This invention soon helped Rome defeat Carthage.

*   *   *   *   *

At the end of the First Punic War, Hannibal's father returned home to Carthage a "hero" but he never forgot the humiliating defeat he and his soldiers had suffered after being ordered by the politicians at home to surrender to the Romans on Sicily.

The story is told how Hamilcar took his four sons (whom he referred to as his "Lion's brood) to Carthage's greatest temple where he made them place their hands on his sword and swear before the idol of Carthage's supreme god *Baal* ("The Lord") that they would never make peace with Rome.

*   *   *   *   *

The sword used in this ceremony, the blade Hamilcar had carried throughout the war, had been passed down through the generations of the Barca family from their ancestor Queen Dido Elissa, the legendary founder of Carthage.

Queen Dido, in turn, had received the sword from her estranged lover, Aeneas, the last surviving member of the royal bloodline of the city of Troy.

This sword had once been the national symbol of the city of Troy and was given to Aeneas for safe keeping by Prince Paris just before Achilles and his "Trojan Horse" destroyed the city.[5]

After the destruction of his city, Aeneas fled to Carthage where Queen Dido immediately fell in love with him and refused to give him permission to leave.

Aeneas told the love-sick Dido whatever she needed to hear in order to buy time until he could escape from Africa to Europe.

According to Roman legend, Aeneas' descendants Romulus and Remus founded the city of Rome in 753 BC.

Maddened by Aeneas' rejection, Queen Dido killed herself with the same Trojan sword Aeneas had left behind in his haste to escape. But before dying, Dido pronounced a curse that her people (Carthage) and the descendants of Aeneas (Rome) would always remain bitter enemies.

*   *   *   *   *

After defeating Carthage in the First Punic War, Rome placed severe restrictions on how big an army Carthage could have, how many ships the city could put to sea, and even restricting what lands Carthage was allowed to trade with and set up new colonies in.

These harsh surrender terms may have been the inspiration for Hannibal's Truth #XLI. As a result of these impossible Roman restrictions, Hamilcar and his sons soon relocated to Spain, which they helped conquer and rule in the name of Carthage.

After the death of his father, Hannibal slowly increased the Barca family fortune and influence in Spain...all the while secretly recruiting a massive mercenary army made up of his own warriors from Carthage, much feared horsemen from Numidia (the African nation bordering

---

[5] This story is told in the 2004 Brad Pitt movie TROY

Carthage), Celtic "barbarians" from Spain, and any other tribe and people who had a grudge against Rome-and there were plenty of those kinds of tribes and people to be found!

Hannibal realized that Rome would not be surprised by any Carthage attack by sea, where Carthage ships might be expected to land troops somewhere along the southern coast of Italy So, instead, Hannibal made his now famous--"impossible!"--march: starting north from Spain, crossing the Alps mountains in southern Europe (in what is now France) to attack Italy from the north, where the Roman border was the least defended.

For the next 16-years Hannibal's army rampaged up and down the length of Italy, defeating all the Roman armies sent against them.

Hannibal was only defeated after going up against another brilliant general, a Roman named Scipio, whose father had been killed in battle when Hannibal had first invaded Italy.

A young soldier himself when his father was killed fighting Hannibal, Scipio spent the next 16 years of his life studying Hannibal's style of fighting.[6]

When finally given command of Rome's Legions, rather than chasing Hannibal's army all over Italy as other Roman generals had done and risk being *ambushed* again and again-as others had been! --Scipio instead stole a page from *Hannibal's* own playbook and instead did an end-run around Hannibal-sailing his army directly at Carthage

With his beloved Carthage suddenly being threatened, Hannibal was forced to abandon Italy and rush home, where Scipio forced him into open battle on the plain of Zama,[7] just outside the walls of Carthage.

---

[6] See Truth #LXXVIII

[7] This famous battle is portrayed in the Roman arena in the 2000 Russell Crowe movie *Gladiator*.

Hannibal had always been wise enough not to face the Roman Legions in open combat, preferring to ambush them with guerrilla-style tactics. Now he had no choice but to face Scipio's Legions on open ground.

Hannibal's defeat at the Battle of Zama brought an end to the Second Punic War.

✷   ✷   ✷   ✷   ✷

For his victory, Scipio was awarded the title *"Africanus"* meaning "conqueror of Africa" (even though he had only conquered *one* city in North Africa.

Keep in mind that at this time, the Romans had no idea how truly vast the continent of Africa really was!

After the war, Hannibal became a *suffete* (political leader) in Carthage, arguing against the harsh terms of surrender Rome was once again forcing on his defeated city.

Worried that Hannibal would start another war, the Roman Senate demanded that Carthage tum Hannibal over to them for trial and execution.

Scipio Africanus argued against punishing Hannibal for his part in the war since he'd come to admire his old foe as an honorable man.

Warned about this treachery, (some believe he was warned by Scipio himself!), Hannibal escaped from Carthage just in time.

Traveling east, Hannibal joined up with another enemy of Rome, King Antiochus of Syria, in his war against the pro-Roman island of Rhodes.

When Antiochus was defeated, Hannibal began operating as a pirate on the island of Crete, attacking any Roman ship that strayed too close.

Stalked by Roman assassins, Hannibal escaped once more, this time offering his services to another of Rome's enemies, King Prusias of Bithynia (modern-day northern Turkey).[8]

However, when the fortunes of war turned against Prusias, the King agreed to betray Hannibal to Rome in exchange for leniency.

At the age of 64, even as Roman assassins were battering down his door, Hannibal defeated his Roman enemies one last time by choosing a warrior's death, falling on his father's sword- the same sword he'd carried all those years ago after first swearing on it in that temple in Carthage.

> "The African is conditioned by the cultural and social institutions of centuries to a freedom of which Europe has little conception, and it is not in his nature to accept serfdom forever. He realizes that he must fight unceasingly for his own complete emancipation; for without this he is doomed to remain prey to rival imperialisms."
>
> ----Jomo Kenyatta, 1938[9]

Key to Illustration 2

A) The City of Carthage's

B) The Battle of Zama (Hannibal defeated, 202 BC)

---

[8] See Truth Llll
[9] Aka Kamau Wa Ngengi (1897-1978), leader of Kenya's *Mau-Mau* secret society/resistance movement.
First President of the independent African nation of Kenya.

C) The Kingdom of Numidia (allies of Hannibal, provided horsemen and elephants)

D) Lands of the Libyans (allies of Hannibal)

E) The Kingdom of Mauritania (alllies of Hannibal)

F) Lands of the Moors (allies of Hannibal)

G) Iberia (modem-day Spain and Portugal, after being conquered by Hannibal and his brothers, many Iberian "Celtics "joined Hannibal against Rome)

H) The river Ebro

I) Gaul (modem-day France, many "barbarian" Gauls joined Hannibal)

J) To Germany, Britain, etc.

K) The river Rhone

L) Luguria (modem-day French Riveria, many Lugurians joined Hannibal)

M) The "impassable" Alps ·

N) The river Po (Rome's northern border)

O) To Greece

P) The Battle of Lake Tresemene (Hannibal victory, 217 BC)

Q) The city of Rome

R) The Battle of Cannae (Hannibal victory, 216 BC)

S) Sardinia (many joined Hannibal)

T) Corsica (many joined Hannibal)

U) The Balearic Islands (many joined Hannibal)

V) Sicily

W) To Phonecia (modern-day Lebannon & the Middle East)

X) To the Kingdom of Egypt

Key to Illustration 3:

A) The city of Carthage

B) The city of Zama

C) To the Kingdom of Mauritania and the lands of The Moors

D) To Celtic Iberia (Spain)

E) To Sicily & Italy

F) To the lands of the Lybia

G) To the lands of the Egyptians

Hannibal's 99 Truths
(an introduction)

"God and history will remember your judgement."

--Haile Selassie Emperor of Ethiopia, 1936

We cannot say for certain where and when, at what time and place in Hannibal's adventuresome life, he wrote his "99 Truths".

Surely, we would err to imagine Hannibal having written these Truths too early on in life, as they are obviously the mature insights of a man who has already "Been there, done that", a man having already witnessed too much of his own people's blood split. Perhaps too, a warrior regretting having seen too *little* of his enemies' blood spilt!

It's not difficult to imagine Hannibal having kept a personal journal, to see him jotting down observations, insights, and revelations as they occurred to him during his travels; with perhaps an anonymous scribe and biographer---African or Roman- finding and editing that journal at a later date.

Most historians are "comfortable" with Hannibal having written his 99 Truths nearer the end of his life; an unrepentant fugitive reflecting back on the joy that had occasionally visited him, and on the hard lessons of life that had been his constant companions--even as the Roman wolves were once again scratching at his door.

But if you come looking for "comfortable", you didn't come looking for Hannibal!

And while tradition argues in favor of it, we cannot say with any certainty why Hannibal chose to "limit" the many insights (and indictments) gathered during his surprisingly long life to only 99?

Some even eye this number "99" with suspicion, accusing it of somehow being symbolic, as if a deliberate slight or challenge by Hannibal to the all-mighty Latin *centi,* the Roman "l00", so important to the Roman way of organizing the world.

For others, *any* numbering of Hannibal's "Truths" is cause for contention, with some experts challenging what they see as artificial divisions having being made by later editors to Hannibal's original pristine verses. They argue for example that commonly-themed thoughts like those expressed in Truths XXIV and XXV would be "easier" to understand if joined together.

But if you come looking for "easy", you didn't come looking for Hannibal! Others argue the contrary: that Hannibal's more lengthy Truths, for example Truth #LX, would be "easier" to understand if divided into 5 or even 6 stand-alone verses.

Again, "easy" and "Hannibal" are not known for sharing the same bed. And, rather than dismissing such arguments as "a tempest in a teapot", we would do better to view any attempt to trivialize or otherwise limit Hannibal's far-reaching appreciations of life in general and his winning applications in particular as more like trying to *catch* a tempest *in a* teapot!

And why call them "Truths" in the first place, instead of simply "Sayings" or perhaps "Meditations", like those of the stoic Roman Emperor Marcus Aurelius.

The answer to this final question is that, whether these 99 were first crowned "Truths" by Hannibal's own hand, or by the heavy hand of an unknown editor much later...It doesn't matter.

When reading each of these "99 Truths", each of us must find a truth to both fit and benefit our individual needs.

It is for this reason we first translate Hannibal's 99 Truths *without comment,* before then presenting them a second time with what we hope is helpful background and interpretation.

For, in the end, each of us must find our own way through life.

And if a single one of Hannibal's "99 Truths" should ease and enlighten our journey through life, then we owe The Conqueror at least *98 more* thanks!

Hannibal's 99 Truths

THE TRUTH ABOUT YOUR ENEMIES & AMBITION

I.

Enemy! When you look at me don't see something you hate.... see the very thing you Jove the most. For that is what I will surely rip from you if you ever rise against me!

II.

We are made as much by our enemies as by your ambitions.

III.

We sometimes win simply because our enemy decides to lose.

IV.

What a man loves, what he hates, what he needs, what he desires: These are the four pillars that support his house.

V.

Distinguish between gain and lose. Nothing you can hold in your hand can ever truly be held for long.

Distinguish between need and desire.

I desire many things. I need few. My enemies can entice me with both of these--drawing me here, sending me running there.

All I truly need beats within my breast. All I desire can all too easily fall into my enemy's coarse hand. The more a man possesses, the more easily he can be possessed.

VI.

A warrior is known by his enemies, even as a fat man is known by his appetites, a lean man by his fears.

I give thanks for my enemy. Were it not for my enemy I would sleep past dawn, I would eat too much, I would become loud and over-proud, and both my arms and eyes would go lax.

My enemy determines when I rise, when and where I sleep tonight, what I eat and when and whether I will ever see my home again.

I thank my enemy for making me strong and look forward to repaying him in kind!

VII.

Give freely to your enemy. Give him a clear and straight path to go down, wish for him a soft bed to sleep in tonight. Pray all his ships find the calmest of seas.

VIII.

The hand guides the blade but the eye guides the hand. The sword is nothing without the hand, the hand nothing without the eye.

IX.

Enemy! My generals keep me awake at night. Your generals keep me laughing during the day!

THE TRUTH ABOUT INTELLIGENCE

X.

Enemy! I watch your every move as if you were the most beautiful of dancing girls: I watch your every step forward and back and to the side, each bend of your knee, every sway of your ample hips. I study every gesture of your hand-closing, opening; the practiced smile of your brightly-colored lips, the wide and narrow of your painted eye.

Soon enough we dance!

XI.

To see only what the enemy shows you makes you his fool! To hear only what your enemy wants you to hear places you in gralledanger.

To look but not to see, to listen but not to hear, this is the beginning of your doom!

XII.

One eye is all you need to see clearly.... if you are truly looking.

A three-legged dog still bites.

XIII.

Do not fear those things you can see, do not be troubled by rumors and loud noises you hear. Fear instead those things you neither see nor hear but that lurk in your enemy's breast!

XIV.

Secrets bleed like blood.

XV.

Mysteries call out to be understood. Every lock longs for a key, every empty cup thirsts for wine.

XVI.

A mystery begins where light ends.

For every mystery laid to rest, another mystery rises. Better the mystery familiar.

For every enemy laid to rest, another enemy rises. Better the enemy familiar.

XVII.

What I know today, my enemy knows tomorrow.

What my enemy knows tomorrow is what I teach him today!

XVIII.

A secret is useless unless someone knows it.

XIX.

The darkest secrets bury themselves.

XX.

A fool begins by telling you what he knows and ends by telling you what he doesn't know.

XXI.

The wise feed off the foolish, but are all too soon hungry again.

XXII.

A wise general must fill his head before he fills his belly. A wise general must fill the belly of his army before he fills their hand.

Hungry soldiers pay more attention to the cook than to their commander. Tired men look more towards the night's sleep than to the day's task.

XXIII.

The weather changes freely to please the Gods.

My enemy's mind changes as it pleases me!

XXIV.

Nature commands me, "Play the actor." So, I play the wave. I don the mask of the wind:

Slowly wearing away my enemy's shore, lazy lapping waves suddenly surge, seizing up and drowning all within reach!

Felt but never seen, the wind gently sways the palms...before suddenly snapping the trunk in two!

XXV.

Nature commands me, "Take this gift of strategy."

So, I study the tracks and droppings of a great beast, I perceive my enemy's passing.

As one beast preys upon another and is in tum preyed upon:

Alert below for food, the kite does not see the threat from above. Likewise, feeling himself general of the sky, the hawk does not see the lowly threat.

In this manner, the striking hawk takes the kite from above while, unseen and unexpected, my arrow takes the hawk from below!

XXVI.

Better an enemy over-bold than a timid one. The former tests my mettle, the latter tests my patience!

XXVII.

Impatience has slain more men than even the best of bowmen.

XXVIII.

Brick-by-brick the patient thief carries away the rich man's house in a single night.

XXIX.

Fear spills less blood. A single scare is worth a thousand cuts.

XXX.

Bleeding my enemy is the next greatest joy to burying him.

XXXI.

I stagger left and my enemy laughs at the "Drunken Man." Suddenly

I strike right! And all laughter ceases! I stumble back, my enemy falls headlong onto my sword as he tries clinging to me.

XXXII.

The patience of sand overtakes all things.

Each thought of man is but a single grain of sand.

Yet a single grain of sand can ruin even the best bowman's aim.

A single grain of sand in the eye can turn the greatest of war-beasts from its tasks!

XXXIII.

A thousand uses for a rock.

A length of wood, a twirl of string, and a skillful hand and kuowing eye crafts a bow.

XXXIV.

Make the ground fight for you.

XXXV.

Today the enemy has a name for *me-Target*.

Tomorrow I will teach him a new name for *me-Master!*

THE TRUTH ABOUT WAR

XXXVI.

War does not feed my sons. But at least it will keep my enemy's sons from eating as well!

XXXVII.

"Do not make war on women and children," the cry.

Why not?

Without his woman's arms to comfort him, his ears filled with the hungry cries of his children, I have twice discomforted my enemy!

XXXVIII.

Waste is worse that war. Never burn a field that may one day feed your own sons.

THE TRUTH ABOUT PEACE

XXXIX.

War should be swift, peace swifter still.

XL.

Peace is a time for sharpening the plow.

Spy out your neighbor's ploy often.

XLI.

The peace should never cost more than the war.

XLII.

It is hard to show an open hand to an enemy. Harder still to show a firm hand to a friend.

XLIII.

So long as my right hand grips the sword and my left hand holds fast to the danger, both remain closed to grasping friendship.

XLIV.

If it began with a word, it can be ended with a word. If it began with the sword, the sword will surely end it.

XLV.

Shame your enemies with your mercy.

XLVI.

Mercy is the most costly of conceits...as if life and death were truly yours to give! The power of life and death is but on loan from The Gods. Use both wisely.

THE TRUTH ABOUT THE GODS

XLVII.

The Gods favor those who first favor themselves.

XLVIII.

The Gods may feast on faith...but they always wash it down with blood!

XLIX.

We all for dance for The Gods' pleasure.

Entertain them well.

There's nothing more dangerous than a bored God!

L.

Trust in the Gods...but always carry a spare sail.

LI.

The Gods choose whom they will...but so too do we choose our Gods!

LII.

The pull of the current, will and warriorhood, and the whim of the

The Gods: These three determine a man's fate.

THE TRUTH ABOUT REVENGE

LIII.

The wine of a true friend is fine indeed. But some thirsts can only be satisfied by the blood of a foe!

LIV.

The nearer the blood, the more it burns.

Blood always tells, but you may not like its tales.

LV.

Revenge should wait until both your sword and your wits have been sharpened.

LVI.

Revenge demands a steady hand and a steadier eye.

LVII.

Revenge demands a long blade...and a longer memory.

LVIII.

Revenge, like fine wine and royal blood, takes time to ferment properly.

THE TRUTH ABOUT HONOR

LIX.

Duty flows out from my heart.

Obligation pours into my ear!

LX.

He who fights for blood soon finds it dripping from his own heart. He who fights for glory never lives long enough to hear the victory songs.

He who fights for gold is already blinded by the glitter and the glare of his own greed, all too soon led astray by all things shiny.

He who fights for sport seldom finds The Gods in a sporting mood. He who fights for love must leave the one he loves the most behind so he can dance with the one he hates the most.

But he who fights for honor cannot be led astray.

LXI.

Skin cut a thousand times eventually heals. Honor wounded but once never heals.

LXII.

War always begins with deceit. This is why war is always the final recourse of an honorable man.

LXIII.

War always ends in desperation and death...and the death of honor is the most tragic of these.

THE TRUTH ABOUT THE NATURE OF PEOPLE

LXIV.

Employ men according to their humors, deploy men according to their fevers.

LXV.

The most treacherous of beasts wears its fur on the inside.

LXVI.

The barking of beasts is a blessed thing...it warns of their approach. Do not fear the noise, fear the silence.

LXVII.

Back-slapping in fat times, back-stabbing in lean.

In lean times, one piece of meat is just as good as another. My enemy's heart is just meat!

LXVIII.

An enemy may blacken your face with blows, but only you can blacken your own heart.

LXIX.

Trust the heart before you trust the skin.

His skin is white but his heart is black.

His skin is black but his heart is white.

All blood runs red.

LXX.

Failure boasts few friends.

There are no feasts at Failure's table, his sons fallen to the sword and to slavers.

LXXI.

The emotions of men shift as surely as the wind and are as unsteady as the shifting sands.

LXXII.

Beware calling another man "genius." A tree always looks tallest when surrounded by shrub.

THE TRUTH ABOUT MAKING YOURSELF STRONGER

LXXIII.

Test yourself with fire and ice, sand and sea, bile and blood, before your enemies do.

LXXIV.

Pain is ever the best teacher.

Pain is only weakness leaving the body.

Death is only pain leaving the body.

LXXV.

A first taste of defeat, though bitter, goes far to prepare your palate for future feasts.

LXXVI.

Discipline is ever an iron trap-be sure you are the one to set it in place.

THE TRUTH ABOUT FAMILY & FRIENDS

LXXVII.

The best hearth doubles as a kiln.

LXXVIII.

No one teaches my sons as well as my enemies.

LXXIX.

All that is required of a father is to teach his sons patience. Sons, by their very nature, teach their fathers patience.

LXXX.

Mirrors tell the cruelest tales.

A good mirror never shows the same reflection twice.

Can you remember your face before we had mirrors?

The face of a friend is the truest mirror.

LXXXI;

The enemy of my enemy is my friend.

LXXXII.

Men are never as helpless, nor ever as clever, as they believe themselves to be.

THE TRUTH ABOUT WIT & WISDOM

LXXXIII.

Wit is the sharpest of swords but the thinnest of shields.

LXXXIV.

The words we weave today bind us to tomorrow.

LXXXV.

Today's lie, tomorrow's test of memory.

LXXXVI.

Truth makes a fine philter but a meager meal.

LXXXVII.

Tradition makes a fine footstool but a poor ladder.

LXXXVIII.

A single thrust to the heart saves a thousand cuts to the limbs.

LXXXIX.

In for a sip, in for a sea.

XC.

Mercenaries at least fight for pay...Fanatics fight for anything. And for nothing!

XCI.

Victors sing the victory songs. Dirges to the defeated.

Which sounds the sweetest of all The Gods?

War cries!

XCII.

No true gift comes with tax, toil, or tail attached.

XCIII.

No shadow walks without some light.

No light that doesn't carry its dark brother.

So with shadows, so with men.

Too much light blinds as surely as too little.

The light of truth never casts a false shadow.

XCIV.

To be thankful for what you have been given, remember what was given up.

XCV.

No spire higher than fire, no ocean deeper than fate.

THE TRUTH ABOUT DEATH & LOVE

XCVI.

My son will die today. My son will die a hundred years hence. My tears will taste the same. Grief does not take notice of the sun's passing.

XCVII.

Death is death no matter from what direction she comes to embrace you.

XCVIII.

Better an early death than a late trial.

Love and death are the only things of value that come
looking for us.

Subject Quick Find

- AESOP (6th century, Black Greek philosopher and story teller, aka
  "The Ethiop"): XXVIII; XLIII; XLVI; XLVII; L; LII; LXXI; LXXVIII.

- AFENI (Black Panther) See "Tupac Shakur".

- AFRICAN PROVERBS & WISE TALES; XLVI (Swahili); LXXII
  ("The 3 Blind Men & The Elephant"); IC (Masai); XXXII (Swahili);
  XXXVII (Kikuyu-Kenyan). See also "Antar".

- ALEXANDER DUMAS (1802-1870, noted Black author who wrote
  "The Count of Monte Cristo") LV.

- ALEX HALEY (1921-1992, author of *Roots,* co-author of *The
  Autobiography of Malcolm* X): XXXV.

- ALI IBN-ABU-IALIB (aka "The Lion of God", 602-661): XLIII

- AMBITION: II

- ANTAR (aka "Abul Fouaris", ancient African hero and king): LXXX.

- ARISTOPHANES (450-385 BC, Greek philosopher): XLIII.

- ARMINIUS (17 BC-21 AD, nemesis of Rome): XLIII; LXXII; LXXIV;
  LXXVIII; LXXIX; LXXXVIII.

- ASSASSINS (Medieval secret society): LXXXVIII.

- ATTILA THE HUN (406-453, Asian conqueror of Europe): XXV; XXXI; XXXVI; XXXVII; XLII; XLIV; XLIX; L; LIV; LXVII; LXXXVIII; IC.

- AYN RAND (1905-1982, philosopher): III.

- BAIBARS EL-RUKN (Egyptian general): See "Mamluks".

- BARACK OBAMA (President of the United States): XXXIV.

- BENJAMIN FRANKLIN (1786-1790, author, inventor, diplomat): XXXVI; XLIII.

- BUDDHA (5th century BC Indian prince & philosopher): V; LXXIV; XCI (Zen).

- BUSHIDO (The Way of The Samurai): LXXXVII; XCVII; See also "Nine Times Down, Ten Times Up".

- BUSTER DOUGLAS (noted African-American athlete): XIII.

- CAO CAO (155-220 AD, noted Chinese commander & strategist), VII.

- CH'EN TU-HSIU (1879-1942, Chinese philosopher): LII.

- CHRIS GARDNER (author of *The Pursuit of Happyness)*: IX; X; LXXXII.

- CLEOPATRA (69-30 BC, Queen of Egypt): Introduction section; X; LXXXI.

- COLIN POWELL (Decorated African-American General): Introduction section: IXX; XLII.

- HAILE SALASSIE (1891-1975, aka Ras *Taffari Makonnen,* honored African Emperor): Introduction section.

- HAMLET: VIII; XLVIII; XCII; XCIV. See also "Shakespeare".

- HASAN IBN SABAH (aka "The Old Man of the Mountain", Assassin Grandmaster & strategist): See "Assassins".

- HENRY FORD (1917-1987, millionaire inventor & businessman): LXXV.

- HENRY 0. FLIPPER (1856-1940, I" Black graduate of West Point, soldier, cowboy, and businessman): XXVII; XXXIV.

- HERODOTUS (485-425 BC, Greek historian, called "The Father of History"): XCVI.

- HOW NOT TO LET YOUR MOUTH WRITE A CHECK YOUR ASS CAN'T CASH! V; VIII.

- HOW TO AVOID "FAIR-WEATHER FRIENDS": LXX.

- HOW TO BE MORE "STREET SMART": X.

- HOW TO GET RICH: XLVI.

- HOW TO KEEP SECRETS: XIV; XV; XVIII; XIX.

- HOW TO MAKE WAR: XXXVI-XXXVIII.

- HOW TO OVERCOME PREJUDICE: XXXIII.

- HOW TO PERFECT YOUR PATIENCE: III; IV; XXVI; XXVII; LXXIX.

- HOW TO SPOT A STRONG WOMAN: XXVI; XXXIII; LXXXVI. See also "Cleopatra"; "Maya Angelou"; "Sister Souljah"; and "Whoopi Goldberg".

---

[10] Played by Forrest Whittaker in the 2006 movie *The Last King of Scotland*.

- MACHIAVELLI (1469-1527, master strategist, author of *The Prince):* II; XXIX; XLIII; LXXXI.

- "MAGIC" JOHNSON (Noted Black athlete): LXXVII.

- MAFIA (aka *la Cosa Nostra,* "This thing of ours"): LIII. See also "John Gotti"; "Lucky Luciano"; and "Scarface AI Capone."

- MALCOLM X (1925-1965, aka "Malik el-Shabazz"): Introduction section; III; X; XXXIV; XLI; XLIII; LVIII; LXXIV; LXXXVII; LXXXIX; XCVIII.

- MAMiti.UKS (Egyptian slave-warriors): Introduction section; XXXV; LXXVIII.

- MAO TSE-TUNG (1893-1976, Chinese revolutionary): LXIV.

- *MASAKATSU!* (Japanese, "By any means necessary!"): XXXVI; LXXVI.

- MAU MAU (African revolutionary secret society): Introduction section. See also "Jomo Kenyatta".

- MGOBOZI MSANE (Zulu General): Introduction section: XCVII; XCVIII. See also "Shaka Zulu".

- MIKE TYSON (Black Heavyweight champion & actor): XXXI; LXXV; LXIV.

- MTUME (Acclaimed philosopher & entertainer): XCI.

- MUHAMMAD (570-632 AD, Prophet of Islam): XI; LXII; LXV.

- MUHAMMAD ALI (Black Heavyweight champion, actor & activist): I; VII; X; XXIV; XXXV.

- MUSASHI (Japanese Samurai strategist, author of *A Book of Five Rings)*: III; X; XIII; XXX.

- NAPOLEON (1769-1821, European conqueror): III; X.

- NAT TURNER (l800-1831, Freedom fighter): XXIX; XXXV; LVI; LXXXIX.

- NELSON MANDELA (African activist & 1st Black President of South Africa): XXXIV.

- NIETZSCHE (1844-1900, German philosopher): VI; XXXIV; XLII; LVII; LXXIII; LXXX.

- NIMROD (aka "Orion", first King on Earth): XCV.

- "NINE TIMES DOWN, TEN TIMES UP". LXX; LXXV; XCV. See also "Bushido".

- OMAR KHAYYAM (1050-1123, Muslim poet and philosopher): IV.

- OMAR THE CONQUEROR (581-644, 2nd Caliph of Islam): XX.

- OMAR (from *"The Wire")*: XXXVII.

- OTHELLO: XXI. See "Shakespeare".

- OVID (Roman philosopher, 43-18 BC) LXXVIII.

- PUBLIUS SYRUS (Roman philosopher): LXIII; LXVIII.

- "REACTION vs. RESSPONSE": XCVII.

- ROBERT CHURCH (1839-1912, first African-American millionaire in The South): LXXV.

- RUSSELL SIMMONS (African-American entrepreneur): Introduction section: X; LVI; LXI; LXVI; LXVII; LXX; LXXII; LXXCVI; LXXXII-LXXXVI; XC.

- SAMUEL L. JACKSON (award winning African-American actor and activist): XXXIV.

- "SCARFACE" AL CAPONE (1899-1947, Italian-American gangster): XXXII.

- SCIPIO AFRICANUS (Roman commander, nemesis to Hannibal): Introduction sections: II.

- SHAKA ZULU (1787-1828, African conqueror & King): Introduction section; I; VII; XXII; XXXIV; XXXVI; XLI; XLV; LUI; LXXXI; LXXXVII.

- SHAKESPEARE (1564-1616, English author): VIII; XXI; LVIII.

- SISTER SOUUAH (African-American writer & activist): XV; LUI; LXXXVII.

- SOCRATES (470-399 BC, the most famous of Greek philosophers): LII.

- SOPHOCLES (496-406 BC, Greek dramatist): XLVII.

- SPARTACUS (died 71 BC, gladiator & slave-revolt leader): VI; VIII; XV; XX; XXXI; XXXII; XXXV; XXXVII; XLVIII; LXXVIII; LXXIX; LXXXI.

- STALIN (1879-1953, ruthless Russian dictator): LXXXVIII.

- SUN TZU (5th century BC Chinese strategist, author of *The Art of War)*: I; II; III; V; VII; X; XI; XVII; XXIV; XXV; XXX; XXXVI; XLIV; LI; LXII; LXXVII; LXXXII; LXXXVII.

- TAVIS SMILEY (Award-winning TV personality and activist): XLIII; LXX.

- "THE THREE KNOWS": IV; LXXXII; LXXXVIII.

- "THE THREE BLIND MEN AND THE ELEPHANT": LXXII.

- TIGER WOODS (Noted African-American athlete): LXXVII.

- TONY DUNGY (Winning African-American Super Bowl coach): LXVIII.

- TOUSSAINT L'OVERTURE (1743-1803, Haitian General and revolutionary): LXXVIII; LXXIX.

- TUPAC SHAKUR (1971-1996, African-American entertainer): XCVI.

- VLAD TEPES (aka "Dracula", Prince and guerrilla strategist): XIII; XXIII; XXV;. aiX; XLIII; LIV; LXXVIII; LXXX.

- W.E.B. DuBOIS (1868-1963, African-American sociologist, educator): IV

- "WHAT DOESN'T DESTROY ME ONLY MAKES ME STRONGER": See "Nietzsche".

- WHOOPI GOLDBERG (Award-winning African-American actress & entertainer): VIII; XXXII; XXXIV; XLIV; LXXXIV; XCVII.

- WHY IT'S IMPORTANT TO TAKE CARE OF YOUR "POSSE": XXII; XXVI; LXXXVII.

- WHY "KNOWLEDGE IS POWER": X.

THE TRUTH ABOUT ENEMIES & AMBITION

I.

Enemy! When you look at me don't see something you hate...See the very thing you love the most. For that is what I will surely rip from you if you ever rise against me!

When Heavyweight Champion of the World Muhammad Ali was asked by a *Sports Illustrated* reporter why he was refusing to be in the United States Army, risking losing his title and risking going to prison rather than go to war in Vietnam, ""The Greatest" responded:

> "Why should they ask me to put on a uniform and go ten thousand miles from home and drop bombs and bullets on brown people in Vietnam while so-called Negro people in Louisville are treated like dogs?"

Ali finished by explaining why the Vietnamese were not *his* enemy:

> "They never called me nigger!"

In other words, never let anyone pick your enemies for you. And, yes, you *do* have "enemies".

Call your enemies "competitors", or "challengers", or "rivals", they're all simply anyone standing in your way, preventing you from getting what you want, achieving what it is you're trying to achieve.

Sometimes you're *physically* confronted by enemies: someone holding on to the championship belt you want; your ex-girlfriend's ex who thinks he knows martial arts; some racist bastard telling you "Your *kind* can't come in here!".

But most times it's a *mental* battle, with the negativity of nay-sayers constantly trying to undermine your feeling of self-worth, draining off your energies and smoking up your resources, using every put-down and dirty trick in the book to prevent you from performing at your peak.

The up-side of this is that *your enemies can make you. stronger*

The stronger your enemy is, the fiercer your competition, the better and fiercer you have to be.

In Truth IV, Hannibal even *thanks* his enemies for forcing him to sharpen his game. But even back in Hannibal's more violent time, *51%* of the game was still *mental:* hoodwinking your enemy, "psyching" your competitor out, making him lose the. game before he ever steps foot on the field.

Sun Tzu's *Art of War* tells us that the *best* enemy is the enemy we *don't have* to fight, the enemy we can convince to turn around and go in the other direction, to throw in the towel before the match ever starts.

The wise Buddha taught the same thing: "Your greatest weapon is already in your enemy's mind."

That's why when *Sports Illustrated*[11] asked football phenome Donte Stallworth (who majored in *Psychology* at Tennessee State, by the way), who was then wide- receiver for the New Orleans Saints, what his favorite motivational book was, you might imagine Donte would have said the Bible, the Koran, or at least the Saints NFL playbook, but instead he praised the mind-control strategies found in a book called MIND MANIPULATION: ANCIENT AND MODERN NINJA TECHNIQUES by Dr. Haha Lung and Christopher Prowant[12]

---

[11] Http://sportsillustrated.com/vault.1230.04
[12] Citadel Press, 2002. Also published as BLACK SCIENCE by Paladin Press, 2001.

Like *all* professional athletes, at least the successful ones, Donte intuitively understood Hannibal's formula that 51% of any game----any *battle---is mental.*

Today everybody's worried about being politically correct, about being "sensitive" to over-sensitive peoples' feelings.

This kind of thinking[13] makes Hannibal's harsh warning to his enemies in this first Truth sound threatening......and that's just what it is.

Your enemies---your competition---should know *fear* before they dare step foot into the ring, onto the court, or out onto the field (be it a football field or a battlefield!) with you.

Machiavelli[14] knew the score:

> "Since love and fear can hardly exist together, if we must choose between them, it is far safer to be feared than loved."

> Why will your enemies fear you? Because they know you've come to *play...and* play *hard!*

Before you can be a "gracious" winner you have to be a *vicious* opponent!

> "Strike an enemy once and for all. Let him cease to exist as a tribe or he will fly at your throat again."

> ---Shaka Zulu (1787-1828)

---

[13] Big word alert: *"Appeasement"*: when you give up and give in, agreeing with someone (Right, like your. girlfriend) just to avoid a fight. A temporary fix, this only makes you look weak in the long run, causing you to lose respect **in the other persons eyes, inviting them to mess with you even more.** "Capitulation11 another big word, meaning pretty much the same thing, especially when spelled "ca-BITCH-ulation!

[14] 1469-1527, *The Prince.*

II.

We are made as much by our enemies as by our ambitions.

Despite what you have been taught, "ambition" *isn't* a dirty word.

And, as already established, neither is having "enemies" necessarily a bad thing. As with most things in life, both "enemies" and "ambition" will benefit you if you're smart enough to take a little time to better understand both.

In his *Art of War,* Sun Tzu warns that "Success has never been associated with long delays Study long, study wrong.

Rome's' war with Hannibal lasted over 16 years.

When Hannibal first came storming over the Alps with his elephants. he caught the Romans by surprise and won several victories. However, the longer the Second Punic War dragged on, the more the Romans *adapted* to Hannibal's way of fighting until, eventually, Scipio Africanus successfully used Hannibal's own tactics against him.

His father's defeat at the hand of Rome in the First Punic War had helped mold Hannibal into the man he became. See Truth LXXXVII.

In tum, ironically, Hannibal helped create and educate the very Roman who ultimately defeated him.

Ask yourself what enemies your actions and ambitions---your needs and wants-are creating today that you'll have to deal with tomorrow? Whether you're digging deep holes or building high towers today, determines which one you'll be sitting in tomorrow.

In China, the *yin-yang* 'symbolizes the balance of opposites: good-evil; light-dark; male-female; hot-cold; inside-outside; etc.[15]

The lesson of the yin-yang is that, in order to find peace and happiness and enlightenment, we must try to find "a balance" in all things.

Simple example: If you're trying to move a heavy piano, having someone pull on it the same time you're pushing · helps move it easier.

Likewise, your "enemies" (the things and people you hate and the things and people who hate you) are always *pushing* at you.

At the same time, your ambitions (the things you want and need) are also *pulling* at you.

So although Hannibal's second Truth points out how we are all influenced-aided or else ambushed!---by both our enemies and by our ambitions, that's not necessarily a bad thing so long as we *recognize* and *admit* to ourselves that these two things do have influence *on* us....but can never be allowed to have control *over* us:

> "The slave has but one master, the ambitious man has
> as many masters as there are persons whose aid may
> contribute to the advancement of his fortune."

> ----J. De La Bruyere

In *Barry Gordie's The Last Dragon* (1985) the young martial arts hero Bruce LeRoy learns the valuable life lesson that "Confusion is part of life, as are vengeance, fear and love."

In the same way, don't let anybody tell you you're not justified in

---

[15] For more on this *Taoist philosophy* see MIND-DRAGON: THE 72 LOST SECRETS OF THE TAO WARRIOR by Dr. HaHa Lung,.

getting angry sometimes, for example when you see a child going hungry or old folks being bullied. It's even natural to feel hate sometimes.

We're supposed to hate things like poverty and evil and injustice. In those cases, *hatin' becomes movivatin',* helping us get up the courage to work towards making things better.

And we've already established how Hannibal was a man who understood the importance of enemies.

One man looks at a mountain blocking his way and sees only an impassable obstacle. Another man looking at that same mountain thinks "That mountain looks like a challenge, climbing that mountain will make me *stronger!"*

Or as the old poem tells us:

> "Two men looked out through prison bars: one saw mud, the other *stars!"*

Take a look at how, in Truth VI, Hannibal gives "thanks" to his enemies for helping keep him on top of his game.

In the saine way that enemies and "haters" can help keep you alert and motivate you to work towards positive change, pushing *and* pulling you closer to your goals, so too your ambitions can help you to focus, to *concentrate* and *coordinate* your thoughts and actions and, when necessary, *conserve* your immediate resources in order to realize your long-term plans, in order to achieve your ambitions.

No. It's *never* easy dealing with your enemies and achieving your ambitions. If life were easy, this planet would *really* be crowded!

* * * * *

"There are two things to aim at in life: first, to get what you want; and, after that, to enjoy it. Only the wisest of mankind achieve the second."

----L. Smith

*   *   *   *   *

"If people don't laugh at you when you tell them your dreams.... then you aren't dreaming big enough!"

-----"MVP", professional wrestler

"The biggest human temptation is to settle for too little."

------Thomas Merton, monk

"If ambition doesn't hurt you, you haven't got it."

-----K. Morris

III.

We sometimes win simply because our enemy decides to lose.

All it takes is patience and a plan.

Sun Tzu's *Art of War* gives us the following formula for success:

"First make yourself invulnerable and then await your enemy's moment of vulnerability."

Likewise, in his 1645 *A Book of Five Rings* master Samurai swordsman Miyamoto Musashi (1594-1645), advises us to adopt a similar *patient* strategy for winning: first perfecting our own defense, while patiently waiting for our opponent to drop his guard.

Of course, if you can come up with a play ' that will *make* your opponent drop his guard or drop the ball, both Sun Tzu and Musashi agree that's even better!

When two equally-matched fighters or players meet, their skill-levels the same, it always comes down to one of them *making a mistake* and the other taking advantage of that mistake.

How many ballgames have you seen where the winner was decided not by a last-second clock-beating throw from half-court or by a quarterback missle into the endzone but rather by someone on the other team stumbling---missing a pass, fouling on a double-dribble to give up a free-throw?

Likewise, chess master J. Redstar tells us:

> "Chess is a game of mistakes, not making any of your own mistakes, while ever-alert for stumbles made by your opponent."

True that.

Following Sun Tzu's advice, and the observation of Hannibal, we keep our own game tight (making ourselves "invulnerable") while patiently---ever alert! ---waiting for our opponent to become "vulnerable" by making a mistake we can profit from.

Following this formula, we have *two* ways to win:

- Our own strength, and

- Our enemy's weakness.

We can only be *sure* of the first, but we can sure *take advantage* of the second! Keep in mind that your *haters* are always out there hatin' and waitin'---and wishing-for *you* to stumble, fall, and fail.

That's why---instead of wasting *your* time hatin' on the haters-you spend your time dotting your "I's" and crossing your "T's", and double-checking the charge in your Smart phone so you'll always be ready when Opportunity knocks...or calls, or texts.

There's an old saying that "Doing well is the best revenge", meaning that nothing pisses off your haters more than seeing you do well, living large.

Another old saying that "Chance favors the prepared mind" just agrees with Sun Tzu and Musashi and with Hannibal: you gotta already have your condom on the minute Opportunity lifts her skirt.

It doesn't make you a bad guy just because you're always ready to scoop up the other guy's fumble and rush into the endzone for the winning touchdown. It makes you The MVP!

All the great generals down through history, down to the present day, have been quick to profit from the mistakes of their enemies.

It's called "opportunity".

And patience creates opportunity.

Born a slave in the French Colony of Saint-Domingue (modem-day Haiti), when the opportunity presented itself, young Francois Toussaint L'Overture (1743-1803) joined the French army.

Despite facing prejudice and cruelty, Toussaint was quick to volunteer for every dirty assignment, every dangerous mission. This young African's "positive" attitude first got noticed and finally earned him the respect of his commanding officers. As a result, Toussaint moved steady up through the ranks, learning all he could, studying his "masters" closely, mastering their art of war.

Encouraged by the young man's obvious intelligence and enthusiasm and by his show of "loyalty", the French offered Toussaint even more opportunities, opening doors normally closed to ex-slaves. Obviously, Toussaint's French "masters" had never heard of Hannibal's LXXVIII Truth, about being careful whose "sons", you train. In other words, of being mindful of what seeds you're sowing today.[16]

Toussasint rose steady through the ranks, until he obtained the rank of General in the French army.

But, all this time, unknown to his French "masters", Toussaint had been *secretly- patiently---training* and arming a rebel army of his fellow slaves!

By 1791, General Toussaint was ready. He launched a slave revolt lasting 2 years, until finally forcing the French to abolish slavery on the island.

Under the terms of the peace treaty the victorious rebels forced the French to sign, General Toussaint, the ex-slave, became the new colonial Governor of Saint-Domingue!

But the French were only playing for time and, in 1802, a large French army again invaded the island trying to reestablish slavery in Saint-Domingue.

Having expected treachery from the French all along, Governor Toussaint L'overture had spent the "peace" preparing for war, building his army even stronger. See Hannibal's Truth XL.

---

[16] For a more modern telling of this same lesson, read Sam Greenlee's *The Spook who sat by the Door* and see the 1973 movie of the same name.

Though Tousssaint died in 1803 (believed assassinated by the French), his "rebel" army went on to defeat the French invaders and, in 1804, Saint-Domingue became the independent nation of Haiti.

Toussaint L'overture's lesson to us:

> Ambition and patience paired with opportunity=success
> over our enemtes.

Another important lesson we can learn from Toussaint L'overture's life is that our actions often have unforeseen consequences, affecting the lives of those around us in ways we can't imagine.

For example, Tousssaint L'overture's actions in Haiti ended *up*helping change the entire world. How?

The fierce resistance Toussaint's "slave" army put up against the French invaders forced Napoleon (Emperor of France who came to power in 1799) to keep sending more and more soldiers to Haiti to fight against the rebels[17]. This drained off Napoloen's military resources in Europe, weakening his warring against other European countries, and ultimately contributing to his losing his throne in 1814.

This drain on France's economy also convinced them to sell all the land they owned in North America. The new United States bought this "Louisiana Purchase" from France and overnight doubled the size of its territory by adding another million acres that today makes up parts of the 15 states in the middle of the country.

Finally, and most importantly for African-Americans, Toussaint's successful-- *bloody!* --*revolt* against Haiti's French slave masters scared the bejesus out of slave owners in the United States and led to the passing of laws stopping Southern slave owners from bringing in any new slaves from Africa.

---

[17] Just like the United States had to do during the Vietnam War in the 1960's and the Russians had to do after invading Afghanistan in the 1980s.

One man with *patience and a plan* did all that!

*   *   *   *   *

"At first man was enslaved by the gods. But he broke their chain. Then he was enslaved by the Kings. But he broke their chains. He was enslaved by his birth, by his kin, by his race. But he broke their chains. He declared to all his brothers that a man has rights which neither god nor king nor other men can take away from him, no matter what their number, for his is the right of man, and there is no right on earth above this right. And he stood on the threshold of the freedom for which the blood of centuries behind him had been spilled."

-----Ayn Rand, ANTHEM, 1938

*   *   *   *   *

"It was the slave revolt in Haiti, when slaves, black slaves, had the soldiers of Napoleon tied down and forced him to sell one half of the American continent to the Americans. They don't teach us that. This is the kind of history we want to learn."

-----Malcolm X[18]

---

[18] *By Any Means Necessary* (Pathfinder,1970:125)

IV.

What a man loves, what he hates, what he needs, what he desires: These are the four pillars that support his house.

Some authorities maintain that Truths IV, V, and VI should be bundled together, since they all deal with "The Three Knows":

- Know yourself,

- Know others, and

- Know your environment.

It's a no-brainer that the more aware you are of your surroundings, and the more you understand about what others around you are up to, then the better your chances of succeeding.

But any way you look at it, Job One is always to *know yourself*, to understand your own motivations, what Hannibal here calls your "loves", "hates", "wants" and "needs".

Most importantly, you need to know how these four drives fit in your life.

Get to "know" yourself before your enemies and all the other haters in the world do, before they learn your attitudes and ambition; using them to jerk your chain and set you off, easily manipulating you.

Get to "know" your environment by paying closer attention to what's going on around you, from knowing what the weather's going to be today, to what's "trending" on the Internet, to what everybody's texting and talking about.

Get to "know" others by seeing yourself in them. This means when we meet people, we either recognize something about them we like ("Hey, they're pretty cool!"; "That's *dope!*;" I have to get me one of those!"; "I have to learn how to bust a move like that!"). Or else we recognize something in that other person that pisses us off and turns us off, some attitude or action that immediately makes us kick them to the curb ("That's so *snake!* As soon as I met him, I just had a feeling he couldn't be trusted!"; "I can't believe she did that!";" That's *whack!* I'd never act like that!").

To know others---your friends and your enemies---as well if not better than you know yourself, requires patience.

You know patience, right? Patience is the door opportunity eventually knocks on. Knowing others opens all door. Remaining ignorant of the loves and hates and wants and needs of others closes doors and---more dangerous still--closes your *mind:*

> "Herein lies the tragedy of the age: not that men are poor--all men know something of poverty; not that men are wicked-who is good? Not that men are ignorant- what is truth? Nay, but that men know so little of men."
>
> ---W.E.B. DuBois (1868-1963)

*   *   *   *   *

By the way, the word "ignorant" comes from the root "to ignore", meaning you're not seeing and paying attention to what you ought to be paying attention to.

"Pay attention now.... or pay the Undertaker later!"

---Dr. Haha Lung

*   *   *   *   *

This Truth is sometimes called "The Four Pillars", with *Love* balancing out *Hate,* our *Wants* balanced against our *Needs:*

- *Love:* Though out of necessity Hannibal lived in violent times, that doesn't mean he was a violent man by nature, or that he didn't know love in his life.

In his various Truths he reveals love and concern for his sons (XXXVIII, LXXIX, and XCVI), for his friends (XLII and LIII), and for lost loves in Truth LX (lamenting having to "leave the one he loves the most" in order to have to go to war). And he `reserves his final Truth for commenting o;rture of both Death and Love.

Love can make you strong when it gives you the strength to do what you have *fo* to help those you love.

- *Hate* is usually the most wasteful, most dangerous of emotions:

    "My life, my *rea/life,* was in danger, and not from anything other people might do but from the hatred I carried in my own heart."

    -----James Baldwin, *Native Son,* 1955

But we've already pointed out how all hate doesn't have to be a negative thing:

    "A good righteous hate gives you a certain amount of focus. But, for the most part, hate makes us act irrationally. That's because, more often than not, so much of our hate is born out of irrational thinking in the first place."

    -------*Mind Warrior,* 2010

In Truth LX Hannibal tells us how to assign men duties according to their temperament and passions, according to "The Four Pillars": what they love, hate, need and desire.

But he then reminds us in Truth LXXI of just how quickly and easily a person's emotions can shift, both the emotions of others, as well as· our own emotions

- *Needs & Wants:* In the following Truth V Hannibal goes into detail explaining the important difference between the things we *want* versus the things we really *need*.

*　*　*　*　*

"Heav'n is but the vision of fulfilled desire."

-----Omar Khayyam, 1123

*　*　*　*　*

For more insights into the motivations of men, see" Hannibal's 6 Movers of Men" in Truth LX.

*　*　*　*　*

"The most potent weapon in the hands of the oppressed is the mind of the oppressed."

----Steve Biko (aka Steven Bantu), 1946-1977[19]

V.

Distinguish between gain and lose. Nothing you can hold in your hand can ever truly be held for long.

---

[19] Written 1979. Died (assassinated?) in prison. cf. "Your greatest weapon is in your enemy's mind."---Buddha.

Distinguish between need and desire.

I desire many things. I need few. My enemies can entice me with both of these---drawing me here, sending me running there.

All I truly need beats within my breast. All I desire can all too easily fall into my enemy's coarse hand. The more a man possesses, the more easily he can be possessed.

Around the same time Sun Tzu was writing his *Art of War in* China, about 500 BC, over in neighboring India a prince named Siddhartha was giving up all his wealth to become a penniless monk

After that, it only took another 40 years fasting and meditating as a monk for Siddhartha to finally figure out the secret:

All people suffer and they suffer because they either want things they don't need or else they want things they can't get.

From then on Siddhartha was known as "The Buddha".

The Buddha had figured out the simple truth that there's what we *need* and there's what we *want,* and that confusing the two is where all our troubles start.

A couple hundred years later, on the other side of the world, Hannibal either read, about what The Buddha had taught, or else he figured it out on his own and made it one of his "99 Truths".

Great minds tend to think alike.

Figure out what you *need....and* never confuse it for what you *want.*

There's nothing wrong with your wanting things or with your wanting things to go your way.

Your "wants" are also your "dreams" and your dreams are what move you ahead through life and help you get ahead in life.

But never let some hustler----whether on the street or on the TV--convince you that you" need" what he's selling, especially when, up until just a minute ago, you didn't know what he's selling even existed!

Here's the key: *Wallet and want have to balance.*

It's okay to have more wallet than want.... that's called being" rich"!

But when you have more want than wallet...well. That's where you start making mistakes, getting in over your hear in debt or, as the Old Folks say, "Letting your mouth (or, in this case, your "want") write a check your ass can't cash!"

*   *   *   *   *

And while on the subject of "wanting" things we can never get: Stop trying to change the past.

You can drive yourself crazy sitting around second guessing about things you shoulda, woulda, coulda done in the past:

- "What if I had done that instead of this?"

- "What if I had said this instead of that?"

That's the past. And there's nothing you can do about the past except admit "My bad", and remember not to do the same whack thing again, not to say the same lame thing again, not to have your headphones turned up so loud you won't hear opportunity knocking *the next time.*

The past is the past, but there was a time when the past was still the future, when yesterday wasn't yet today.

But today is today. Right now. And tomorrow is still" the future", and so you still have time to do something about it.

Tomorrow doesn't have to be like yesterday or even like today. It *can* be better. Don't let the haters tell you different.

If you want to be stronger tomorrow, you need to hit the gym *today.*

If you want to have a little more phat in your bank account tomorrow, you need to get your hustle or your education---or why not *both? --on today.*

If we had prepared better yesterday, we'd be doing better today. What are you doing *today* to prepare for *tomorrow?*

Your dreams stay dreams until you start crawling out of bed *before* the other guy does.

> "Your Wheel of Fortune is not a game of chance. It is a game of choice. You will spend your life by the choices you make. There are no timeouts, no substitutions, and the clock is always running."
>
> ----Dennis Waitley, SEEDS OF GREATNESS, 1983

*   *   *   *   *

> "Dreams may be all you have right now, but they are the doors you walk through to a better life."
>
> -Isaiah Thomas, 2001

VI.

A warrior is known by his enemies, even as a fat man is known by his appetites, a lean man by his fears.

I give thanks for my enemy. Were it not for my enemy I would sleep past dawn, I would eat too much, I would become loud and over-proud, and both my arm and eye would grow lax.

My enemy determines when I rise, when and where I sleep tonight, what I eat and when and whether I will ever see my home again.

I thank my enemy for making me strong and look forward to repaying him in kind!

———————————

Slave-turned-gladiator-turned-rebel leader Spartacus tells us:

"The wind in my face only strengthens my step."[20]

Likewise, in his 2001 autobiography *The Fundamentals: 8 Plays for Winning the Games of Business and Life.*[21] basketball great Isaiah Thomas tells us how "grateful" he is for having grown up on the tough streets of Chicago:

"You develop keen instincts in a neighborhood where life and death are part of the day to day.... What didn't destroy me made me stronger[22] whenever I've faced a

———————————

[20] For all the wisdom and warrior strategy of this slave-turned-gladiator-turned-rebel leader see" The War Scroll of Spartacus" in Dr. Lung's *Lost Arts of War* (Citadel Press, 2012).
[21] HarperBusiness,2001:76.
[22] Thomas here is making reference to bad boy philosopher Friedrich Nietzsche (1844-1900) and his oft-repeated declaration:" What doesn't destroy me makes me stronger" See also Truth LXXXVII.

challenge since then, I've been able to draw strength from the fact that what I dealt with and survived as a boy was far more challenging."

While you are supported by our family and friends, you're *challenged* by our competitors, challenged to make yourself stronger and faster and smarter:

> "Tropical fish placed in a barren bowl remain lethargic. That is until you place a simple rock in the bottom of their bowl. Then our little finny cousins will swim around and around that rock until l their little flippers fall off.... So every morning when you wake up (if only because you probably wouldn't the alternative), thank The Gods, thank Mother Nature, your selfish and xenophobic DNA, and even Nietzsche for tossing a few rocks into your fishbowl....*Mind Warrior*[23]. See also Truth LXXIII.

VII

Give freely to your enemy. Give him a clear and straight path to go down, wish for him a soft bed to sleep in tonight. Pray all his ships find the calmest of seas.

Where Hannibal's Truth VI told us how we first need to make ourselves stronger (SW1 Tzu's "First make yourself invulnerable...."), this Truth now tells us how to weaken our enemies (" await your enemy's moment of vulnerability.") by giving him everything he wants.

---

[23] See "Why you Need to *rock* Your World" in *Mind Warrior* by Dr. HaHa Lung and Christopher B. Prowant (Citadel Press, 2010.).

Remember how, in the 1990 movie *Goodfellas,* assassins were able to draw the normally paranoid Joe Pesci character into a trap by offering the one thing he wanted the most: to become a" made man" in the Mafia?

Thus the old rule that "When an offer sounds too good to be true, it probably is!

Schemers always tell you exactly what you *want* to hear to get you where they want you to be, to get you to do what they want you to do.

Chinese strategist Cao Cao (155-220 AD) tells it this way:

> "Offer your hungry enemy meat to draw him out of his house.[24]

The best example of Hannibal himself putting this Truth into practice was at the Battle of Cannae, where his much smaller army beat a much bigger Roman army men by giving the Romans exactly what they *thought* they wanted: a face-to-face fight with him.

For months Hannibal had frustrated all the Roman armies sent after him by *avoiding* them, by refusing to give them a "fair" face-to-face fight. Instead he fought hit-n-run guerrilla-style: with small groups of his men sniping at the Romans, then quickly disappearing before the Romans had a chance to respond, making the Romans "chase" Hannibal all over Italy.

Finally, Hannibal stopped "running" on the wide-open plain of Cannae, where the Romans assumed their feared Legions would be at an advantage.

Falsely thinking they had trapped Hannibal, the Romans charged directly into the "envelopment" trap Hannibal had set.

The Battle of Cannae was the greatest defeat in Roman history.

---

[24] See "Cao Cao's Nine Strategies" in *Mind Warrior,* 2010.

Two thousand years later Shaka Zulu (1787-1828), creator of the Zulu Empire in southern Africa, adapted Hannibal's "envelopment" maneuver into his" Cow's Horn" strategy, first drawing his enemies in by pretending to retreat, before suddenly surging forward to surround and crush them![25]

Boxing master Muhammad Ali used the same strategy in the ring: first tiring his opponent's by making them "chase" him around the ring, frustrating them with his famous "Rope-a-Dope, drawing the unsuspecting "dopes" closer in....before suddenly unleashing a devastating counter-attack!

Any time you can get an enemy competitor to underestimate you, they are going to make mistakes and drop their guard.

Isaiah Thomas likewise touched on this same strategy in his 200 I autobiography, first cultivating his own skill, while always on the lookout for any "weakness" shown by his competitors:

> "The most competitive of athletes, like Larry Bird, have highly refined predatory instincts. They play at a heightened level of awareness and they can sense mental letdowns as well as physical weakness in an opponent." (Ibid.)

VIII.

The hand guides the blade but the eye **guides the hand, the sword is nothing without the hand, the land nothing without the** eye.

---

[25] For more on the life of Shaka Zulu, see Truth LXXXVII.

When Hannibal uses the word "eye" in Truth he's talking about us not just "looking" at a situation, but our learning to actually "see" what's going on beneath the surface; to not just "hear" what someone's saying, but to "listen" to what they're *really* saying, and to what they're *not* saying.[26]

What they're *not* telling you---those important details they're leaving out---might just turn out to be more important than that game they're trying to run on you.

In her 1997 *Book*[27], Whoopi Goldberg first warns us to be in the look-out for this kind of "lying by omission", before she then gives us the tried-n-true formula for spotting it:

> "But if you just shut up and let people talk, they hang themselves. They hang themselves."

It's kind of like watching magician David Blaine: you can *look* at what he's doing and even watch him closely, but you still don't really *see* what he's doing and ----suddenly! ---he's got that hot babe floating in the air or he's made a full-grown Bengal tiger appear out of nowhere!

You run into the same kind of problem when you don't *really listen* to what people are saying.

When you're listening to people talk, pay attention not only to *what* they say and to what they *don't,* but also to *how* they say it,

Five- hundred years ago, in his play *Hamlet,* William Shakespeare pointed out how sometimes a person's words don't fit their actions, warning players to:

> " Suit the action to the word, the word to the action..."

---

[26] "Words rule the world. So, rule your words."---The War Scroll of Spartacus. See also Hannibal's Truths LXXXIV and LXXXV.

[27] Yeah, that's the whole title!

It's called" body language"[28]

Have you ever been listening to someone talk when you get this "funny feeling" that "something's not right"?

What's going on is that, while the person's mouth is saying one thing, their body is saying something else.

You're subconsciously picking up on the fact that their "body language" doesn't fit their words:

- She keeps licking her lips, adjusting her clothes, and looking to the right when she swears on a stack of Bibles, she hasn't seen her ex in a month of Sundays. Yeah, she's been up to no-good.

- That street punk's smiling all-friendly, trying to talk you up while his eyes keep darting left and right and he keeps nervously wiping his sweaty hands on his pant legs. Yeah, he's up to no-good.

Trust your "gut-instinct" when you get feelings like this.

Truths XI, XII, and XIII that follow all deal with helping us "see" better.

* * * * *

A second meaning of this Truth is that you have to put your money where your mouth is. Or, as Prince Vlad Tepes[29] pointed out:

---

[28] For a complete course in" body language" see Lung & Prowant's *Mental Dominance (Citadel Press, 2009).*

[29] Vlad Tepes (1431-1476) was the ruthless real-life warrior-prince on which the fictional *Dracula* was based. For all 72 of Vlad's "Certainties" see" Blood Tells: Dracula's Dark Art of War in Dr. Lung's *Lost Arts of War* (Citadel Press, 2012.

"Thoughts are not required of action, but action is required for greatness."

So, don't talk smack unless you can back it up.

And never let your mouth write a check your ass can't cash!

IX.

Enemy! My generals keep me awake at night. Your generals keep me laughing during the day!

Whereas a "good" enemy helps keep us on our toes and makes us stronger (Truth VI), sometimes those who care about us the most, our family and friends, inadvertently hold us back, undermining our plans, preventing us from achieving our goals by draining our energy.

A lot of the time our loved ones do this by accident, by not paying attention to what they're doing, or else because they're truly trying to" help us".

Sometimes they stand in our way because they're worried, we're "dreaming too big", that we're going to fail, fall, and hurt ourselves in the process.Often these "well-meaning" people have failed themselves in the past and have been disappointed in their own lives and are now trying to "protect us" by preventing us from f ling similar pain from experiencing similar failure.

But we're not them. And just because someone "means well" doesn't mean they *do* well.

All too often, thinking to save us from disappointed and harm, they stand in our way.

In his Truth XLII Hannibal recognizes this and tells us that, no matter how hard it is to stand your ground against a friend or family member, sometimes you just have to *firmly* tell them to step aside and allow you to take the chance-- the calculated risk-that's going to bring you one step closer to your dreams.

This may sound "harsh", but you're not going to be much good to other people until you get your own self organized.

When it comes to other people, even loved ones, wasting your time and money, you have to be firm, standing your ground and keeping your eyes on the prize. This means deliberately ignoring the petty distractions of others, even those people you love.

Of course, others are going to think you're "selfish" and maybe even accuse you of being "cruel" when you *prioritize* this way. And sometimes you'll just have to put up with their complaining about you being a selfish S.O.B. until you achieve your goals. Then you'll be in a better-stronger--position from which to help those very same people-family and friends-who were standing in your way.

In his autobiography *The Pursuit of Happyness*[30], entrepreneur and motivational speaker Chris Gardner gives us 44 lessons for helping us realize our goals, the final lesson of which is that we must *claim ownership of our dreams* which, like everything else in life, comes with a price:

> "There is a cost, absolutely, when you decide to be in charge of your own unlimited possibilities. The freedom to choose your destiny does indeed come with a price---responsibility." (Ibid)

Nobody rides for free.

---

[30] Made into the hit 2004 movie starring Will Smith.

THE TRUTH ABOUT INTELLIGENCE

X.

Enemy! I watch your every move as if you were the most beautiful of dancing girls: I watch your every step forward and back and to the side, each bend of your knee, every sway of your ample hips. I study every gesture of your hand-closing, opening; the practiced smile of your brightly-colored lips, the wide and narrow of your painted eye.

Soon enough we dance!

The fact you're reading this book means you already know that *knowledge is power.* Still, it never hurts to be reminded: "Knowledge is power."

----Sir Francis Bacon (1561-1626)

"Knowledge is the frontier of tomorrow. Brain is becoming more and more the master of brawn."

----Dennis Waitley, SEEDS OF GREATNESS, 1983

"Your mind is your greatest weapon. It's great when you're a good shot with an AK. -47, but it's about being clever."

---V.P. Wilson, former-CIA agent

Learn from anyone and everyone. True knowledge is all about snatching up every bit of "intelligence" you can from anyone and everyone you can.

Don't let any personal *preference* or *prejudice* get in the way of you increasing your odds of success by increasing your overall knowledge, no matter where that knowledge might come from.

At the beginning of the 2nd Punic War, the European Romans were "prejudiced": already convinced in their own mind there was nothing an "uncivilized" African commander like Hannibal could teach *them when* it came to making war.

In short order, Hannibal taught them different.

This prejudice[31] the part of the Romans almost cost them an empire! Because:

> "Any prejudice can cause us to dismiss potential teachers out of hand because of their race, religion, gender, or culture. A truly wise man learns from both friend and foe."
>
> -------Lung & Prowant, *Mind Contro/2006*

Hannibal, on the other hand, was always willing and eager to learn from anyone and everyone, from friends and from his enemies (see Truths II, XIV, XX, etc.), and even from Mother Nature (see XXIV, XX, etc.).

*   *   *   *   *

Cleopatra, (69-30 BC), Queen of Egypt, was another African ruler willing to learn from anyone, even from invading Europeans.

Cleopatra was only 16 when her father Pharaoh Ptolemy XII died. Soon after.J Cleopatra's enemies within the royal court staged a *coup* in

---

[31] From the root meaning" to pre-judge", to make a decision about something or someone *before* getting all the facts.

the name of her 10-year old brother and the young queen was forced to flee for her life.

But unlike those traitors who had just ran her out of Egypt, Cleopatra saw "The Big Picture". She realized that, even when she regained the throne of Egypt-and there was no doubt in her mind she *would* regain her throne! --there was still an even bigger threat to *Egypt-Rome*.

Having realized in his own time that Rome was the biggest threat to Egypt, Cleopatra's father Ptolemy XII had prepared his daughter for dealing with this potential threat by educating her well in the language and customs of Rome.

Now realizing she needed help from Rome to reclaim her throne, Cleopatra had one of her servants secretly wrap her up inside an expensive rug and carry her to the Roman leader Julius Caesar as a gift.

When Caesar unrolled the rug, out popped Cleopatra!

Impressed by how a young girl had out-smarted all his security, dazzled by her beauty, Caesar couldn't help but fall in love with Cleopatra....as she had *planned* all along:

> "Whatever skills Cleopatra may have had in the area of lovemaking and cosmetics were supplemented by her keen intelligence, education (she is said to have known seven or eight languages), and deep understanding of people."
>
> ---*Power: The Ultimate Aphrodisiac*[32]

"Borrowing" Caesar's army, in a short time, Cleopatra regained her throne. After Julius Caesar was assassinated in 44 BC, Cleopatra then seduced and manipulated the new Roman leader Marc Anthony.

---

[32] "Dr. R. Westheimer with Dr. Steven Kaplan (Madison Books,2001)

Because of her knowledge of Roman thinking and customs (which allowed her to manipulate Roman leaders), Cleopatra was able to keep control of her kingdom when so many other kingdoms around her were being conquered by Rome.

For over 20 years Cleopatra controlled Egypt, North Africa, and much of the Middle East. She was also influential in the internal politics of Rome itself. All of this because she had taken the time to learn all she could about a potential enemy, turning that potential enemy into an ally.

*   *   *   *   *

A Book of Five Rings by Japanese sword master Miyamoto Musashi (1594-1645) is second only to Sun Tzu's *Art of War* for mastering Eastern martial arts strategy.

Musashi taught his students to "Learn the Ways of all professions," learning from anyone and everyone they could because you never know what particular piece of knowledge might come in handy.

The more you're willing to learn today about life in general, and about your enemies in particular, the better your chances of living to see tomorrow.

You hear people argue about the difference between being "book smart and being street smart". Well, there's nothing wrong with being *street smart...as* long as it's *Wall Street smart,* like Donald Trump and Russell Simmons!

When asked how he had conquered half the world, Napoleon replied, "All my victories begin *in the library!"*

That's the reason why Southern slave owners prevented their slaves from learning to read and write. As writer Joel Chandler (1848-1908) tells us through his character *Uncle Remus:*

"Put a spelling-book in a nigger's han's an dar' you loozes
a plow hand."

And that's why Chris Gardner early on put learning at the top of his
list of ways to succeed:

"When my brain wanted to give up, my attitude was that
I had to study like I was in prison----because knowledge
was power and freedom. An image rode along with me
of Malcolm X in prison, teaching himself by studying
the dictionary starting with "aardvark"."

----*The Pursuit of Happyness,* 2006

Isaiah Thomas, no slacker himself in the brains department, also
under stood that, whether in sports or in business, it's all about the"
mind game", taking his inspiration from boxing great Muhammad Ali:

"Muhammad Ali's mind games sometimes defeated his
opponents before he even threw a punch."

(Ibid. 2001:139)

And recall how Dante Stallworth's favorite book wasn't called Grab
the Football and Run Real Fast! it was called *Mind Manipulation* (Citadel
Press, 2001).

⋆   ⋆   ⋆   ⋆   ⋆

"I am learning all the time. The tombstone will be my
diploma."

-----Eartha Kitt, (1927-2012),
singer, actress, the *first* "Cat woman"
(beating out Halle Berry by 40 years!)

XI.

To see only what the enemy shows you Makes you his fool!

To hear only what enemy wants you to hear places you in grave danger.

To look but not to see, to listen but not to hear, this is the beginning of your doom!

Having convinced us of the importance of gathering up-to-date knowledge, Hannibal's Truth XI, XII, and XIII now offers us ways to increase our intelligence--- both the kind of intelligence you're born with, and the kind you *should* go out of your way to find.

Some experts maintain that these three Truths should be joined together, since they all instruct us on how to "see" more clearly...while at the same time telling us how to become more expert at hoodwinking our enemies.

In his *Art of War* Sun Tzu tells us that "All warfare is based on deception." This is true whether the type of "warfare" you're engaged in is taking place on the battlefield, in the boxing ring or on the basketball court, or in an executive boardroom.

It's always been the rule that "The strong take from the weak, but the *smart* take from the strong."

This is why Sun Tzu reminds us that the best battle is the one we *don't* have to fight, that it's always better when you can *fool* an enemy instead of having to *fight* him---better to pull the wool over his eyes than to have to close the casket lid over his face.

You fool your enemy by making him "see" what *you* want him to "see".

One pitch-black night when his much smaller army was suddenly in danger of being surrounded by a much larger Roman army, Hannibal tied torches to the horns of a herd of cattle and stampeded the animals towards the Romans.

Seeing and hearing all those torches thundering towards them, the Romans were tricked into thinking Hannibal had somehow found reinforcements and was now attacking them with a much larger army.

The Romans ran like Hell!

Likewise, before attacking a much larger enemy force, the Prophet Muhammad had the women in his caravan drag branches behind them, stirring up even more dust, making the enemy think the Muslim fighting force was larger than it really was.

Like Sun Tzu, Muhanunad was fond of saying. "War is deception."

Hannibal tells us more about this method for making our enemies "see" what we want them to "see" in his Truth XV and again in Truth XXXI's "Drunken Man" strategy.

*   *   *   *   *

"Appearances are often deceiving."

-----Aesop "The Ethiop"

XII.

One eye is all you need to see clearly...if you are truly looking.

A three-legged dog still bites.

Everyone's favorite story of all time, told and retold in every culture in every time, is the story about some poor guy who is beaten down, crippled up, maybe thrown into prison, sometimes even left for dead, who not only survives against impossible odds but ultimately succeeds in turning the tables on all his haters, perhaps even coming back to get revenge against all those who plotted against him.

We find this lesson over and over in The Bible **in** the stories of Joseph and Samson and David; in Muhammad's flight to freedom and eventual return in triumph to Mecca; from fictional stories like *The Count of Monte Cristo;* to true-life stories of the heroes of the Underground Railroad, Malcolm X, and Hurricane Carter.[33]

The lessons to learn from all these stories is, first

- *Never underestimate your enemy.*

A dying man can still have enough fight left in him to take you out with him!

The second lesson here is:

- *Never underestimate yourself*

You're doing things *today* you never dreamed you were capable of doing *yesterday*. What dreams of *today* are gonna carry you into *tomorrow?*

No matter what time and resources you may presently lack, whatever pieces are "missing" from your plan right now:

---

[33] See the 1999 Denzel Washington movie *The Hurricane.*

Never let what you don't have keep you from getting what you will have.

While fighting in Italy, Hannibal was wounded many times and even lost an eye. But he didn't let this "handicap" slow him down.

On a spiritual level, the "eye" has always been the symbol of wisdom and power. That's why the Freemasons put the "All-Seeing Eye" of the Egyptian God Horus on that pyramid that's on the back of every American dollar bill. "See" also Truth XX.

"You go on or die."

----Harriet Tubman, 1820-1913,
"Conductor" on the Underground Railroad

XIII.

Do not fear those things you can see, do not be troubled by rumors and loud noises you hear. Fear instead those things you neither see nor hear but that lurk in your enemy's breast!

In Japan, Miyamoto Musashi taught his sword students to practice and meditate in order to develop *mekurc*[34], "the inner eye", a kind of Samurai warrior "ESP", where Musashi's students learned to "sense" what their opponent was about to do. This is what Musashi was talking about when he wrote:

"When you cannot be deceived by men you will realize the wisdom of strategy."

---*A Book of Five Rings*, 1645

---

[34] **Pronounced "me-cure-ah".**

But while it's a great idea to develop a *mekura* "sixth sense" to give yourself a heads up on what your competition might be planning to do next, you can't afford to let your imagination run wild:

- *Never overestimate your enemy,*

Buster Douglas says no matter how big and scary your opponent is... he *can* be beaten! And:

- *Never overestimate yourself.*

You have to keep it real-and that means *paying more attention*[35], to what your enemy is really capable of, and to how capable you really are of "seeing" what he's really up to.

> "All Masters agree: To see with senses alone is not to "see".
>
> ---*Mind Control, 2006*[36]

> "As a rule, what is out of sight disturbs men's minds more seriously that what they see."
>
> ----Julius Caesar, *The Gallic War*

Even kings and princes subject to this "fear":

> "I do not fear the grumbling of the people...I fear their silence."
>
> ---Prince Vlad" The Impaler" Tepes[37]

---

[35] "Pay attention now. Or pay The Undertaker later"--Dr. HaHa Lung.

[36] Written by Dr. HaHa Lung Lung & Christopher B. Prowant. (Citadel Books, 2006).

[37] "People should not fear their government, government should fear their people" ---*V for Vendetta (2006)*

See also Truth LXVI

* * * * *

"In my estimation, fear is the most common obstacle that stands in our way or holds us back from our highest aspirations."

-----Chris Gardner, 2006

XIV.

Secrets bleed like blood.

Truths XIV, XV, XVI, XVII, XVIII, and XIX all deal with the making and the breaking of secrets (with perhaps XX and XXI thrown in to remind us how often secrets spill out the mouth of "Fools").

No secret stays a secret forever.

Benjamin Franklin warned" Three can keep a secret if two are dead." Just look at what all the low-life high society celebrities, rich sports stars, politicians, even Presidents are caught doing: lying, embezzling money, cheating on their wives.

Now if rich and powerful people like that get caught because they can't keep a secret, what chance do you think the rest of have of getting away with it?

5-0 loves to say that "All criminals *want* to confess". What 5-0 means by this is that criminals love to *brag,* even to the point of playing around with the police-playing around with the *po-lice! --about* how smart they are, about how 5-0 will never catch "whoever" *really* did commit the crime because "whoever" really did it is so slick....

Yeah, cops call this kind of *telling on yourself* "duping delight": You talkin' 24-karat crazy cause you think you're The Teflon Don!

By the way, the *real* "Teflon Don", Mafia Godfather John Gotti, died in prison because he liked seeing his picture in the newspaper too much. What's *that* tell you?

Duping (pronounced "doo-ping") delight is why some numb-nuts are so stupid they actually *record* themselves committing crimes on their cell-phones and sometimes even post those videos to The Internet.

Big surprise: 5-0 knows how to use Facebook and YouTube too! America's *dumbest* criminals strike again.

But keep in mind that "criminals" are just the ones who keep quiet. Quiet as it's kept, *everybody* likes to brag. See Truth XX.

* * * * *

"Existing in the spotlight means you have to adjust to the glare."

-----Tavis Smiley,2011[38]

XV.

Mysteries call out to be understood. Every lock longs for a key, every empty cup thirst for wine.

---

[38] *Fail Up* Smiley Books/Hay House, Inc. 2011.

The lessons of this Truth are two-fold.

First, this Truth reminds us that no door is "too solid" that there isn't a key that can be used to open that door.

If you can't get to that key, get to the guy or gal that's got the key. No obstacle, no matter how big, is" too big" to stop you for long if you're determined to get past it:

> "The course of your life is determined by whether you
> buy into your aspirations or your desperation."

> ---Isaiah Thomas

The best example of this Truth is the story of how, when crossing the Alps, Hannibal's army was stopped by a huge fallen boulder blocking their way through a narrow canyon.

Since the rock was too huge to break up with hammers alone, Hannibal had fires built around the rock, heating it white-hot before then pouring gallons of cold wine on it, causing the rock to suddenly crack in a dozen pieces!

In some versions of the story, Hannibal and his soldiers first *drank* the wine before then "pouring" it onto the hot rock.

A hundred and fifty years later, Sparatcus would use this example to inspire his fellow gladiators to rise up and slay their Roman slave-masters:

> "It is said determined Hannibal broke the great rock
> blocking his way with but fire and piss. Can we do less
> with blade and blood?"[39]

This Truth then gives us two gifts of strategy for manipulating an enemy:

---

[39] See "The War Scroll of Spartacus" in Dr. HaHa Lung's *Lost Art of War* (Citadel Press, 2012)

Since "Mysteries cry out to be understood..." and since all people are naturally curious, give your enemy a "mystery" to occupy his time, one calling out to be "understood".

Keep him guessing to keep him busy.

Then, every now and then, let him *guess right,* let him win a hand just to keep *him----and his money! ---in* the game.

Inflate his ego by making him think he's "special", that he can "see" something or figure something out no one else can. (This is how *cults* trick people into joining up!)

Giving your enemy such easy" false victories" will make him grow "cocky" (overconfident) and will encourage him to make mistakes when it really counts.

> "Before slavery, we as African people had understanding and answers for most of life's basic questions."
>
> ----Sister Souljah[40]

XVI.

A mystery begins where the light ends.

For every mystery laid to rest, another mystery rises. Better the mystery familiar.

For every enemy laid to rest, another enemy rises. Better the enemy familiar.

---

[40] *No Disrespect,* First Vintage Books editions/Random House,1996.

Any general or ball coach will tell you there's nothing better than having a *predictable* opponent, one who does the same thing over and over.

Next best to this is having an opponent who tells you what he's up to without realizing he's telling you what he's up to.

If you play ball with the same crew every day, pretty soon you get to where you can predict every move, they're going to make. In the same way, they get to where they can predict *your* every move too.

Likewise, if you play Texas-Hold 'em with the same cast of characters every time you get to where you can read them like a comic book, recognizing all their itchin', twitchin', and bitchin' that "tells" you what kind of poker hand they're really holding.

That's why you've got to be constantly *updating* your own game-- adding new moves, adding new fakes to your play to make your opponent commit left while you ball right!

That's also what Hannibal is talking about in Truth XXXI.

*   *   *   *   *

"I think it pisses God off if you walk by the color purple in a field somewhere and don't notice it."

--Alice Walker, *The Color Purple,* 1982

XVII.

What I know today, my enemy knows tomorrow.

What my enemy knows tomorrow is what I teach him today!

Chapter 13 in Sun Tzu's Art of War is dedicated to spies and spying. Spying out the other guy's secrets while jealously guarding your own.

Being in the right place at the right time and paying good enough attention to spy out the right piece of information before your opponent does is what spells the difference between winning and losing.

Hannibal's father lost the I" Punic War because Romans were in the right place at the right time to capture a stranded Carthage battleship and figured out how it worked well-enough to construct battleships of their own.

During Hannibal's own fighting in Italy, battles were won and lost on both sides because of traitors and spies betraying secrets.

If you have an idea for a new invention, a new product, or even a new song or movie screenplay idea-Go *for it* and *Go for it now!*

You snooze you lose! If you don't act quickly when you get a valuable piece of intelligence, somebody else will beat you to it. That's one of the cold, hard facts of life we have to live with.

This is what Wall Street's all about: buying and selling stock *before* the other trader does, buying stock or selling a particular stock because you've just gotten hold of a piece of information that your competition doesn't have yet (for example, selling stock in a company that's about to go bankrupt, or finding out about a new area where they're gonna start drilling for oil, etc.).

Or, closer to home, how about you're in Vegas getting ready to lay a bet on your favorite NBA team when your brother-in-law the cop texts you that your team's best player just got thrown in jail for DUI and isn't going to be able to make the Play-offs! Think that piece of information is gonna make the bookies change their odds? Better hurry up and lock your bet in on the more favorable odds they're still giving *now!*

See Truth XL.

*   *   *   *   *

"It is thrifty to prepare today for the wants of tomorrow."

----Aesop, "The Ethiop"

XVIII.

A secret is useless unless someone knows it.

Remember that 1989 Will Smith movie *Enemy of the State?*

Yeah, it's like that now *for real.*[41]

Just assume you're on camera wherever you go, whatever you're doing. And even when there's not a camera you can see on every street corner and in every corner of every corner convenience store you stop by, one of your so-called "friends" probably feels compelled to capture every moment of *your* life on his or her Smartphone. (Not all *that* "smart" when you think about it. Right, America's Dumbest Criminals again!).

If you have a secret, there's a pretty good chance that secret is not going to stay secret for long.

Digging up other peoples' secrets is big business nowadays.

---

[41] See *Mind Mafia: How Conmen, Cults, & Government Conspiracies Get Inside Your Head! By Dr. Haha Lung* •

Haters. 5-0. Private detectives and paparazzi. Everybody and their window-peeping granny's getting paid to eye your keyhole, pick through your garbage, and even false "friends" you on Facebook.

Any time a politician gets caught with his pants down or some Wall Street big-wig gets caught with their hand in the cookie jar, they can afford to hire an expensive public relations firm to put a positive "spin" on whichever of their skeletons has fallen out of their closet. So, at worst, they get a slap on the wrist and get re-elected.

The rest of us, we're pretty much on our own when any of our dark secrets come to light.

The best way to take away a secret's power is simply to reveal it before one of your haters gets a chance to.

Or, when your secret's exposed, just *come clean.*

The *Latin*[42] for coming clean, for admitting you made a mistake and taking responsibility, is *"Mea culpa"* (may-ah-kull-pa), a fancy way of saying "My bad."

Once the cats out of the bag, a secret becomes useless.

Once your secret is out, it's" old news", and no one can hold it over your head.

Like a dollar, you can only spend a secret once.

> "That old truism "Nothing spreads like word of mouth," has become obsolete. The Internet is now word of mouth--on steroids. Technology has accelerated the power to inform and destroy a zillion times faster than words we let slip between our lips."
>
> ------Travis Smiley, 2011

---

[42] Language spoken by the ancient Romans, still used by slick-talking lawyers today.

XIX.

The darkest secrets bury themselves.

Ever heard that "Karma's a bitch"?

Karma is the East Indian word warning how all that foul you're putting out is going to come back to bite you square on the ass!

The Bible says "Whatsoever a man's soweth, so shall he reap". Same thing. "What goes around, comes around." Same thing again.

"The darkest secrets bury themselves." is Hannibal's way of reminding us we're all too often our own worst enemy, that, like a dumb-ass, we all too often plant the seeds of our own destruction.

Every one of us has secrets. We keep secrets at our own risk. It's like holding on to a time-bomb. Sooner or later...Boom!

The good news is that this same Truth works for *-against-your* enemy.

All that venom your haters are spitting in your direction? It's all just "bad karma" that's going to boomerang back and catch up with them sooner or later.

And, yes, sometimes you can *help* their "bad karma" catch up with them!

＊　　＊　　＊　　＊　　＊

"I don't have any of those cute little tricks some people like to play to test loyalty. I also don't expect people

I deal with to be saintly or to make sacrifices for the privilege of being in my comer. What I do expect is for people to be honest about their self-interest."

-----Evander Holyfield, 2008

XX.

A fool begins by telling you what he knows and ends by telling you what he doesn't know.

Omar ibn al-Khattab (581-644), the 2nd Caliph of Islam who conquered a fair size piece of the world once wisely observed that there are four things you can never get back:

- An *arrow* that you've already shot from your bow;

- *Time* that you've already wasted;

- An *opportunity* that you fail to take advantage of; and

- Every *word* that ever came out your pie-hole[43].

So, whether you get your philosophy from a rebel slave leader like Spartacus: "Words rule the world. So, rule your words."[44]

Or from Charlie Chan:

"Tongue often hangs man quicker than rope."

---

[43] See "By the Blade and by the Book: Omar in Command" in *Mind Warrior (Citadel Press, 2010)*
[44] See "The War Scroll of Spartacus" in *Lost Arts of War* (Citadel Press, 2012)

It still all comes down to Grandma's old saying that:

"It's better to remain silent and be thought a fool than to open your mouth and remove all doubt!"

* * * * *

WHY DIDN'T SOMEBODY TELL ME?

By 2006 *The Oprah Winfrey Show* was being watched in 130 countries by over 14 million people a day.

XXI.

The wise feed off the foolish, but are all too soon hungry again.

_____

When has there ever been any future in listening to fools?

But if you're forced to listen to fools, don't allow yourself to get distracted by what they're saying. Instead, listen to what they're *not* saying.

In Shakespeare's 1565 play *Othello, his* title character is a Black Moor commanding the army of the city of Venice, Italy, who is driven mad with jealousy and ultimately murders his faithful White wife Desdemona, all because he made the mistake of listening to the lies and innuendo told him by his "trusted" lieutenant Iago (who was secretly jealous of Othello's success).

If you can't sit still long enough to watch Lawrence Fishburne in the traditional 1995 movie version of *Othello,* at least take time to check out the modern retelling of the story of *Othello* in the 2001 movie "0", where a Slack basketball recruit Mekhi Phifer runs afoul of racism in a fancy all-White school.

✳   ✳   ✳   ✳   ✳

In any operation, plan, or project, having truthful up-to-date "intelligence" is job one. This means (1) using all the "intelligence" you were born with, meaning brains, and (2) gathering all the "intelligence" (information) you get by keeping an eye on what your competition is up to.

In any situation you can only go with what you know. You can only act on the information you have on hand.

For now, use both the brains you were born with, and all the information and experience you pick up along the way-and *update* that information every day!

Put what intelligence you have to good use now and The Universe will give you more to work with.

When you get more, *do more.*

And, when you get better-do *better.*

XXII.

A wise general must fill his head before he fills his belly.

A wise general must fill the belly of his army before he fills their hand.

Hungry soldiers pay more attention to the cook than to their commander.

Tired men look more towards the night's sleep than to the day's task.

————————————

A good "posse" works both ways.

Take good care of your posse and your posse will take care of you.

Ever wonder how it is those dusty crusty 100-year old sex-crazed heroin-using hotel-room trashing' rock-n-rollers from the 1960s are even still alive, let alone still able to get up on stage and perform every night for hours at a time"?

It's because, back in the day, they had-and still have-a good *posse:* a loyal crew they came up with who take care of them, who steer them away from all that tempting shorty jailbait, sober 'em up, stick a guitar in their hand and shove them out on stage every night...so *everybody* can continue to get paid.

Like any good commander, Hannibal knew he had to put his posse first, making sure, his men were well-bed and well-fed before he put a sword in their hand and pointed them in the direction of the nearest Roman.

Once Hannibal's soldiers-his posse-realized he was putting their care and concerns first and foremost, they became loyal to him for life.

Hannibal knew the ultimate truth:

Family and friends are what life's all about.

And if *you* don't know this by now...you're probably reading this while sitting in a prison cell somewhere!

See Truth XLV for Shaka Zulu's thoughts on this.

XXIII.

The weather changes freely to please The Gods.

My enemy's mind changes as it pleases me!

Hannibal's next three Truths, XXIII, XXIV, and XXV all deal with the strategy of "the unexpected", being prepared for the unexpected when it happens, and always doing the unexpected ourselves in order to keep the competition guessing-and guessing *wrong!*

*　　*　　*　　*　　*

How easily the mind of a man can change-for the better, for the worse". In Truth LXX Hannibal's scorn for "fair-weather friends" is obvious.

The fact that Hannibal points out the obvious, that "The weather changes freely..." is just his way of reminding us that we should always be ready for the unexpected.

Hannibal then tells is how easily he can change his enemy's mind whenever it pleases him. In anyone else, this would just be talking smack, but Hannibal has the track record to prove it.

What he's telling us is that we need to *take command of the chaos* in order to always be ready to not only set a big bowl of "unexpected" on our enemy's table, but also, be ready to force-feed it to him when necessary!

Confusion is only confusion if you don't see it coming. Otherwise it's called "opportunity".

Whether it's "confusion" or "opportunity" depends on who lights the fuse! Some people use what's called "C.H.A.O.S." to get what they want. They Create Hardships and Offer Solutions. In other words, they (secretly) create the problem in the first place knowing people will have to come begging to them for the solution to the problem.

> This makes them look like a genius and a hero rather than a shit-starter. "The nature of man is to seek rest, food, and fornication. Offer these to your foe in abundance."

> -----Vlad "Dracula" Tepes

* * * * *

WHY DIDN'T SOMEBODY TELL ME?

In 1163, Abd ai-Mu'min, Muslim leader of the Berbers of Morocco drove the last Europeans, the Norman French, out of North Africa.

Europeans didn't return for over 300 years, when the Portuguese began The Middle Passage slave trade.

XXIV

Nature commands me, "Play the actor." So, I play the wave. I don the mask of the wind:

Slowly wearing away my enemy's shore, lazy lapping waves suddenly surge, seizing up and drowning all within reach!

Felt but never seen, the wind gently sways the palms•..**before suddenly snapping the trunk in** two!

If ever any of Hannibal's Truths should be joined together, it would be this and the following two "Nature" Truths. Together, these give us the perfect strategy for influencing---Okay, *manipulating! --the* minds of our enemies.

This follows Sun Tzu's teaching:

> "When you're still a long way away from your enemy, make him think you're getting close. When you're already close by, don't let him know. Instead, make him think that you're still far away and not yet a challenge to him."

This is just more of what you already know to do: Always keep your enemy guessing: Make him think you're still far away in order to "rock him to sleep", giving him a false sense of security.

Or else you make your enemy paranoid by making him think you're already breathing down his neck, before you've even started to make your play.

*   *   *   *   *

"Float like a butterfly, sting like a bee."

--Muhammad Ali[45]

XXV.

Nature commands me, "Take this gift of strategy." So, I study the tracks and droppings of a great beast, I perceive my enemy's passing.

---

[45] Saying devised by Ali aide Drew "Bundini" Brown.

As one beast preys upon another and is in turn preyed upon:

Alert below for food, the kite does not see the threat from above. Likewise, feeling himself general of the sky, the hawk docs not see the lowly threat. In this manner, the striking hawk takes the kite from above while, unseen and unexpected, my arrow takes the hawk from below!

———————————

This Truth reminds us how important it is to pay attention, for two good reasons:

First, you need to pay attention so you can recognize and fully use the resources around you.

Sun Tzu devotes a whole chapter in his *Art of War* to what he calls "Terrain", meaning the lands and the people you'll have to pass through on your way to getting where and what you want.

Back in Sun Tzu's day this meant a general had to figure out how to get his army over real mountains and across real raging rivers-like Hannibal did when crossing the Alps with his elephants.

This is also the kind of really dangerous "terrain" that southern slaves escaping north along The Underground Railroad had to overcome.

But those escaping slaves didn't only have to worry about climbing over mountains and swimming across rivers, they also had to keep looking over their shoulder for the bounty hunters hot on their trail.

So "terrain" can also mean all the people you run into along the path you're traveling through life who will either help you or else get in your way and try to stop you.

That's why you need to keep in mind that "terrain" isn't just the *physical* obstacles in your way, it's also a *"mental* game" you've got to win.

That's why you always need to pay attention to your surroundings:

1. Where you're starting from;

2. Where you're headed (meaning what your goal is); and

3. What kind of "terrain"--places and people--you're gonna have to pass through to get where you're going.

It's not enough to only know which cross-town bus you've got to catch or what gang-infested 'hood you've got to pass through to safely get where you're going. On a bigger level, you have to figure on and factor in the kinds of situations *and people* you're going to have to deal with on your way to the top, on your way to getting what you want.

For example, if you live in a "good" neighborhood going to school and getting a decent education is a piece of cake.

But what happens when you live in a 'hood or barrio where gunfire keeps you awake all night and where you have to jump fences and take short-cuts through back alleys just to avoid all the• bullies, crackheads, and trailer-trash meth-monsters between you and that school?

Education opens doors. But if you can't navigate your way across "enemy terrain" to make it to school...doors start closing.

Sometimes this "enemy terrain" isn't the mean streets.... it's the *meaner* people, all that nay-saying from haters.

It doesn't matter!

You can't let *anything* or *anybody* stand between you and what you have to do, to get where you have to go, to get what you want.

You have to get over that "terrain" if you want to get over in life.

How? By learning to recognize and use the resources (including people)

closest to you, what Hannibal calls "Nature".

Another intractable enemy of Rome, Attila the Hun also knew how important it was to pay attention to--and take advantage of. -any opportunity "Nature"--your surroundings--offer:

> "Men never listen enough. They do not hear what the hawk and the wind and the changing of the seasons would tell them."[46]

So, you pay attention to your surroundings and to the people in those surroundings in order to better protect yourself and your loved ones.

Remember: No matter how long your fangs, no matter how sharp your claws, no matter how hungry you might be, you're never the *only* predator in the jungle!

*   *   *   *   *

"Value force only in proportion to its limitations".

----Prince Vlad "Dracula" Tepes

XXVI.

Better an enemy over-bold than a timid one. The former tests my mettle, the latter tests my patience!

---

[46] **"The Answers of Attila"** in Dr. Lung's *Absolute Mind Control*.

This, and the following two Truths emphasize the importance-uses and misuses--of *patience*.

First up, a predictable enemy, even if a bold enemy, makes it easy for us to win battles. But an enemy that's *too* predictable can actually make us weaker.

This goes back to Hannibal's Truth XXII where he cautions us how important it is to have a good "posse", to always have someone watching your back, someone you can fly your latest scheme by in order to get an *honest* opinion.[47]

There's an old saying that "Behind every successful man there's a strong woman." This is true.

A strong wife, girlfriend, even just a strong female friend can all help make a man, stronger by "balancing" out his natural "If I can just kick enough ass everything's going to turn out all right" nature.

Most "cliques" and street crews revolve around one strong-natural--leader who's surrounded by a bunch of weaker wannabees all trying to come up by kissing' the main man's ass. (Thus, the tried-n-true tactic: "Cut off the head and the rest of the snake dies!")

Strong opponents can make you strong and keep you on your toes by forcing you to come up with even more clever and unexpected moves.

Your muscles aren't going to be any bigger tomorrow if you're lifting the same weight today that you did yesterday. See Truth LXXIII.

If you're not careful, soft and petty enemies can make you soft and petty. So, stay out of petty arguments with petty people.

Just as you're "known by company you keep", you're also known by the people you *argue* with.

---

[47] See also Truth XLII.

Here's the rule:

- We learn from our *superiors* (those who know more about a subject than we do):

- We teach our *inferiors* (those who know less than we do):

- But we only argue with our *equals*.

Any time you catch yourself arguing with someone, ask yourself, "Is this man my *equal*?" If not, don't waste your breath!

*   *   *   *   *

"The superior man will not manifest narrow-mindedness or the want of self-respect."

----Mencius, Chinese philosopher, 372-289 BC

XXVII.

Impatience has slain more men than even the best of bowmen.

Patience is power.

Back in the antebellum[48] south, slaves would often sabotage the plans and projects of "Mister Charlie"[49] by deliberately working slower.

---

[48] Before the Civil War.
[49] The generic name slaves used for all slave owners.

The codename for this delaying tactic was "CPT", "Colored People Time". The man (or woman) who can afford to *stall,* forcing others to wait on their arrival, waiting on them to make a decision, always has the upper hand in *any* negotiation.

Some people do this because they're confident **in** their own ability and position, for example, because they don't "have to have" whatever thing or idea you're trying to sell them.

Other people hold up progress just because they're petty. This is what psychologists call being *passive-aggressive:* deliberately "slow-walking'" you just because they can.

Patience is the key for winning any argument, for wearing down your opponent's "gas", for spying out any weakness **in** a competitor. And for proving your own worth.

Youngsters are always in a hurry to move up before they're really ready to step up. This is called going off "half-cocked"...in *both* ways!

You gotta pay your dues.

Harry 0. Flipper (1856-1940), whose father and mother were slaves, was the first African-American to graduate from West Point Military Academy (in 1877).

Flipper went on to serve in the United States Army out west where he became a much-feared Indian fighter.

During his life Flipper was also an author; a legal consultant and money manager; a mining engineer; and even a Special Agent for the United States Department of Justice.

Here was a man who knew all about "paying dues". Thus, when Flipper heard a younger African-American soldier who was eager to command impatiently complaining about he wasn't being "promoted" fast enough, Flipper patiently took the young man aside and patiently explained to him:

> "The men who have commanded divisions in an army have first commanded a company, then a battalion, a regiment, a brigade, and then possibly he will be fit to command a division."[50]

In other words, before you can make other men sweat, you first gotta *sweat yourself*

*   *   *   *   *

"If you don't have confidence, you'll always find a way not **to win.**"

---Carl Lewis, Olympic champion

XXVIII.

Brick -by-brick the patient thief carries away the rich man's house in a single night.

Impatience is weakness.

Aesop (whose name means "Ethiop of Africa") was a Black slave who lived in ancient Greece around 550 BC. He won his freedom by becoming the most famous story telling philosopher of his time.

---

[50] *8/ack Frontiersman: The Memoirs of Henry O. Flipper.* Texas Christian University Press, 1997:150.

It's from Aesop that we get the fable of "The Tortoise and the Hare", the story of how a slow-moving-but *patient-turtle* ends up beating a fast-moving rabbit in a race because the over-confident *smack-talking* rabbit thinks he's so far ahead of the turtle during the race that he decides it's ok to take a nap till the turtle catches up. But, while the rabbit is still sleeping, the turtle ends up beating him to the finish line!

Thus, Aesop finishes his story by advising us:

"Slow and steady wins the race."

Why "waste" your time studying the wisdom of a bunch of old, dead blowhard Greeks with names like Aesop, Sophocles, Aristotle, Socrates and Plato?

In his 1995 *Black Lies, White Lies: The Truth According to Tony Brown*[51] award-winning African-American television journalist and author Tony Brown reveals the African origins of the original *Pelasgian* (Pelasgoi) Greeks:

> "Some researchers believes that these earliest inhabitants of Greece were a dark-skinned, brown-complexioned combination of groups; Phoenician Canaanites from Asia Minor and Palestine, and Egyptians and East African." (Ibid. p. 133)

Brown points us to Martin Bernal's 1987 *Black Athena*[52] which explains in detail how the ancient African origins of Greek civilization were obscured by Aryans (nowadays called "Indo-Europeans") who invaded into Greece around 600 BC.

Vlad Tepes (1431-1476), the real-life prince who was so feared by his enemies that history remembers him as the fictional "Dracula", learned to be patient while a young prisoner of his Muslim enemies for 6-years,

---

[51] William Morrow and Company, Inc. NY.
[52] Rutgers University Press,1987. Voll.New Brunswick/NJ 1987:79

before he became powerful (and ruthless) enough to take his kingdom back. He gives us the formula: "Single steps, correct or sinister, lay the stones that pave our way through life.[53]

WHY DIDN'T SOMEBODY TELL ME?

Lucius Septimus Severns, Emperor of Rome from 193-211 AD was born in *Africa*.

WHY DIDN'T SOMEBODY TELL ME?

There have already been 3 Black Popes ruling the Catholic Church:

St. Victor I (189-199); Melchiades (311-316); and St. Gelasius, 492 AD[54]

XXIX.

Fear spills less blood. A single scare is worth a thousand cuts.

Southern slave masters *ruled by fear.*

After Nat Turner's 1831 slave revolt those same slave masters *lived* in *fear!*

Born into slavery in 1800, Nat Turner secretly learned to read (when it was still illegal to teach slaves to read).

---

[53] See "Blood Tells: Dracula's Dark Art of War" in Dr. Lung's *Lost Arts of War* (Citadel Press, 2012)
[54] Anderson, 1997:129.

Inspired by what he read in The Bible to become a preacher, in 1831 he led 70 other slaves to revolt, killing 60 Whites in Virginia, starting with his own slave master.

More Whites died in Nat Turner's revolt than in any other slave revolt in U.S. History.

Eventually Turner and 20 slave rebels were captured and hanged. Another 100 innocent slaves were also murdered in revenge by *angry-fearful*-Whites.

Fear of more slave uprisings swept through the south! Laws were immediately passed limiting the number of slaves that could be brought from Africa. New laws were also passed regulating the conditions (food, housing, etc.) under which slaves could be owned.

Read *the Confessions of Nat Turner.*

In Truth LXXIV Hannibal tells us that "Pain is ever the best teacher". But it seems *fear* does a pretty good job too!

$$* \quad * \quad * \quad * \quad *$$

In 1461, a massive Islamic army under the command of Sultan Muhanunad II of Constantinople in Turkey invaded into eastern Europe, including into Transylvania, the Christian kingdom of Vlad Tepes, aka "Dracula"[55]

Unable to fight Muhammad's massive army head-to-head, Prince Vlad and his men wisely took to the hills, determined to fight a guerrilla campaign against the invaders.

Lacking the warriors and weapons needed to openly fight the invaders, Vlad fell back on the one tactic and tool he had plenty of: *fear.*

---

[55] The Name means "Son of the Drago'(Dracul), often mis-translated "Son of the Devil".

Arriving in the first Transylvanian town controlled by Prince Vlad, Muhammad was confronted by the rotting corpses of over 10,000 Muslims and traitors crucified and "impaled"[56]• See *Theatre of Hell: Dr. Lung's Complete Guide to Torture*[57]".

At the next town Muhammad was confronted by 20,000 more impaled corpses, and in a third town, 30,000 more[58]•

At the sight of all these tortured souls-some still alive and begging to be killed just so they could be put out of their misery! --terror swept through the ranks of the veteran Islamic invaders.

Muhammad II, an otherwise brave man who had personally fought in many bloody battles during his life, was so sickened by the sight that he quickly retreated.

From then on Vlad Tepes was known and feared as "Vlad the Impaler".

*   *   *   *   *

An enemy or competitor who fears your ability and likely retaliation is unlikely to pick a fight with you.

Nobody likes to get their ass kicked.

This is why Machiavelli says it's *better-safer--for* a prince to be feared than loved. Because, whereas love can turn to hate in an instant, once you put fear into a man's heart it usually stays put!

---

[56] Where a long heavy wooden pole is shoved up through the victim's anus, expertly avoiding vital organs along the way, until the stake comes out through the person's mouth. The other end of the stake is then driven into the ground and the victim is left to dangle on the stake, sometimes suffering for days before finally dying.
[57] (Loom panics Unlimited, 2003)
[58] See *Children of the Matrix* by David Icke, 2001:126.

Forcing your enemy to make decisions when he's afraid usually works to your advantage. Why? As isaiah Thomas points out: "Decisions made out of fear are almost always wrong." (Ibid. 2001) Your enemies don't have to "fear" you *physically*.

They can also fear your education, your mad skills and expertise, your determination and your drive:

> "Make three correct guesses consecutively and you will establish your reputation as an expert."
>
> *--The Peter Prescription, 19 72*

XXX.

Bleeding my enemy is the next greatest joy to burying him.

This Truth teaches two lessons: First, the *power* of patience and, second, how even the most "impossible" of challenges can be overcome by breaking that challenge down into smaller, more manageable "sub-goals" to be accomplished one-one-one, accomplishing your final ultimate goal:

> "[S]mall successes pave the way for broader undertakings. Accomplishing sub-goals helps bring our grand goal more clearly into view.... Having accomplished your goal, resist temptation to rest on your laurels, to pat yourself on the back and go on vacation. Instead, start *rebuilding* the bridges you burned on your way to the top. Smooth over some of those feathers you ruffled on your way to becoming cock-of-the- walk. Or, as Hannibal

the Conqueror instructed: "Shame your enemies with your mercy."[59]

-----Dr. Haha Lung, *Mind Sword*, 2012

*   *   *   *   *

"I take great personal pride in dreaming big and achieving big, the biggest achievement of all is to be able to help another human being."[60]

----Gene Simmons, *Me Inc.,2014*

*   *   *   *   *

In his *A Book of Five Rings* (second only to Sun Tzu's *Art of War* in Far Eastern strategy classics), Japan's greatest swordsman Miyamoto Musashi teaches this same lesson, calling it "Cutting-at-the-edges".

When a Samurai was unable to defeat a rival swordsman with a *coup de main* direct thrust, he cut at an enemy's arms and legs, weakening ("bleeding") his enemy until able to deliver a *coup de grace* killing blow.

*   *   *   *   *

"The reason we have a "back-up plan" is so we never have to back up!"

·-*Mind Sword*, 2012

*   *   *   *   *

---

[59] Truth #XLV.
[60] **immigrant, entertainer, millionaire entrepreneur, founder of the rock-n-roll group *Kiss*.**

Unable to catch AI Capone drivin' dirty, unable to attack (arrest) him directly for masterminding the Saint Valentine's Day Massacre, and for controlling all Chicago's illegal alcohol, gambling, and prostitution, the Feds finally used "Cutting-at-the-edges" and sent Big AI to Alcatraz for *not paying his taxes!*

"In our time and culture, the battlefield of life is money.

Instead of horses and chariots, guns and fortresses, there banks, checkbooks, credit cards, mortgages, salaries, the IRS. But the inner enemies remain the same now as they were in ancient India or feudal Japan: fear, *self-deception, vanity, egoism, wishful thinking, tension, violence."*

----Jacob Needleman
Money and the Meaning of Life, 2015

XXXI.

I stagger left and my enemy laughs at the "Drunken Man."

Suddenly I strike right! And all laughter ceases!

I stumble back, my enemy falls headlong onto my sword as he tries clinging to me.

In his *Art of War,* Sun Tzu advises:

"When strong appear weak. When weak, create the illusion that you are strong."

Appearing "weak" (or drunk and confused) makes your enemy (1) underestimate you, and (2) *overestimate* himself.

A student of the Sun Tzu system, Li Chung (803-852) tells us:

"Dodge left, strike right. Dodge right, strike left. Fake an attack forward to cover your retreat. Pretend retreat... before springing forward with ferocity!"

Still another Sun Tzu admirer, alcoholic poet named Li Po, created the ancient Chinese style *of "Drunken Monkey Kung-fu",* a martial art using deliberate bobbing and weaving to make it *appear* the Drunken Monkey fighter is drunk and stumbling, in order to make his opponent *underestimate* his ability to defend yourself.

It's always to your advantage when your opponent, competition, and enemy *underestimate* you.

Remember Muhammad Ali's "Rope-a-Dope" maneuver of "falling back" on the ropes, making his opponent think Ali had run out of gas, while actually allowing his opponent to wear himself out...before Ali suddenly-unexpectedly---counter attacked!

Sun Tzu: "All warfare is based on deception."·

Likewise, the Muslim Prophet Muhammad taught: "War is deception." Therefore, anything you can do to make your opponent, your competition, your enemy *underestimate* you, works to your advantage.

General Robert E. Lee: "Bluffing is a legitimate tactic."

∗   ∗   ∗   ∗   ∗

In both the book and then movie of Greenlee's 1960's Black Guerrilla classic *The Spook Who Sat by The Door,* inner city freedom fighters use the tried-n-true guerrilla warfare tactic of tricking National Guard units into chasing a few "fleeing" guerrillas into an *ambush* by a larger group of hidden fighters.

*   *   *   *   *

"When the other guy's army is bigger than your army, and you're fresh out of Hannibal's and Patton's, it's time to go guerrilla on his ass!"

----Dr. Haha Lung, *Mind Sword,* 2012

*   *   *   *   *

"If the tiger stands still the elephant will crush him, so the tiger never stands still."[61]

----Ho Chi Minh

XXXII.

The patience of sand overtakes all things.

Each thought of man is but a single grain of sand. Yet a single grain of sand can ruin the best bowman's aim, a single grain of sand in the eye can turn the greatest of war-beasts from its task!

"War-beast" in this Truth is often translated "elephant". However, since *words*-like any good *sword! ---often have two edges,* Hannibal

---

[61] 1890-1969. Guerrilla leader, then President of North Vietnam.

111

may have also meant this as a metaphor for Rome, that "greatest of war-beasts."

Most importantly, this Truth is a *warning* for us to pay attention to *details*. This was one of Musashi's main instructions to his students: "Pay attention even to triffles.", based on Sun Tzu's warning that *great* and *successful* people always take care of little problems *before* they become big problems.

"You'll never achieve 100 percent if 99 percent is okay."

--Will Smith, rapper, actor and entrepreneur.

*   *   *   *   *

"Respect your bestial birthright. We were petty prey struggling to survive in an unforgiving world long before we evolved brains big enough and ruthless enough to elevate us to the rank of Prime Predator."

----Lung & Tucker
Nine Halls of Death, 2007

*   *   *   *   *

"Life is a competition. Like it or not, you will always be in competition with others."

-----Gene Simmons, *Me, Inc.* 2014

*   *   *   *   *

"Be a Darwinian apex predator---whatever your environment, adapt to it. Conquer it." (Ibid.)

XXXIII.

A Thousand uses for a rock.

A length of wood, a twirl of string, and a skillful hand and knowing eye crafts a bow.

Prejudice means to "pre-judge", to make a decision without first having all the facts, or at least without having enough information to make an "informed guess".

Prejudice also means seeing only one use for an object, a tool, or a person. A rock is only a rock until you can't find your hammer.

When it comes to sizing up people, *prejudice* always errs on the side of *underestimating* them.

For example, *prejudice* made the Romans underestimate Hannibal. And Hannibal made them pay a dear price for their prejudice.

Prejudice also made people underestimate Whoopi Goldberg's chances of ever "making something" of herself.

Credit where credit is due: Whoopi got hers the hard way, never giving in to the shitty hand and hard knocks life had dealt her.

In addition to literally winning *every major* entertainment award possible: A Grammy (for records), an Emmy (for TV), and a Tony (for being on Broadway), in 1990 she won an Academy Award (an "Oscar") for her role in the movie *Ghost* and then went on to be the first African-American woman to host the Academy Awards, in 1994. This is how she explains her success:

"I believe I belong wherever I want to be, in whatever situation or context I place myself [because] I believed a little girl could rise from a single-parent household in the Manhattan projects, start a single-parent household of her own, struggle through seven years of welfare and odd jobs, and still wind up making movies. You can go from anonymity to Planet Hollywood and never lose sight of where you've been...So, yeah, I think anything is possible. I know it because I have lived it."[62]

The Romans initially *underestimated* Hannibal because they *overestimated* their own defenses: No one could march as army cross the Alps, let alone an army that included war-elephants!

How did Hannibal reply to this, including to nay-sayers within his own camp?

"If we can't *find* a way, then we will *make* a way!"

Hannibal wasn't being stubborn. He was just thinking outside "the box" the Romans were trying to keep him in.

The Romans *underestimated* Hannibal's determination.

He surprised them in more ways than one. Who is *underestimating* you right now? Surprise them.

XXXIV.

Make the ground flight for you.

---

[62] *8ook,* Rob Weisbach Books/William Morrow and Company, Inc. 1997

It's always nice to have "home court advantage".

Ideally, home court advantage includes picking the time and the place a competition (or confrontation!) is going to take place.

Truth XXXIV deals first and foremost with how (and *why)* we pick our battles and how we should, whenever possible, be the one who picks the battlefield.

Remember how Momma taught you to "Never let the other kids pick your friends for you." Wise advice.

Likewise, a wise general never lets the enemy pick the time and place of the battle.

When Hannibal advises "Make the ground fight for you" he's not only talking about the way, in his time, a general had to know the "lay of the land", for example whether he'd be marching and fighting on flat land or mountains, in winter snow or in summer heat.

Once a general knew these things, he could then plan how to use them to his advantage.

The modern example of this is your taking full advantage of all the *benefits* of your surroundings---whether ghetto or graduate school-have to offer, making full use of opportunities open to you while collecting all payment due you.

Know what you got coming. *Get* what you got coming.

West Point's first African-American graduate Henry 0. Flipper lamented:

> " No civilized people is so ignorant of their Constitution
> and functioning of their government as the American
> people, and this ignorance runs all the way from the

college graduate to the most illiterate clodhopper."
(Ibid.)

You paid your taxes and God knows you've paid your dues---paid in sweat and blood and tears.

You're not asking for a *handout,* you're asking for a *shout out,* a long overdue

"Thanks" for helping build this country from the ground up.

You say you grew up in a "bad" neighborhood, or come from the "wrong side of the tracks"? Turn that to your advantage, turn a negative into a positive, like so many before you have done.

Like so many others, Barack Obama came from a single-parent home.

Like so many others, Whoopi Goldberg escaped from the seductive sinkhole of welfare.

Like so many others, award-winning actor Samuel L. Jackson overcame drug and alcohol addiction.

Like so many others, Isaiah Thomas refused to become yet another victim of the violent streets just outside his window.

> "When you grow up poor and black, you learn to value every opportunity to better your position in the world, and you develop an ability to find opportunities in the most unusual places.....Given that my neighborhood had far more sinners than saints, I had to become a selective shopper in the role model market. Some of my tarnished boyhood role models may have had rap sheets instead of resumes, but there were still worthwhile things to be learned from them." (Ibid)

Malcolm X, Nelson Mandela, and countless others stepped onto the path to greatness while still in prison. That's about as deep into "enemy territory" as you can get! And yet they made that "ground" work for them.

Nietszshe said "Whatever doesn't destroy me makes me stronger." Perhaps he should have also said *"Wherever* doesn't destroy me makes me stronger."

*　*　*　*　*

WHY DIDN'T SOMEBODY TELL ME?

In March 1896 Rome (now the Kingdom of Italy) again tried to invade Africa.

10,000 Italian soldiers were killed and another 18,000 scattered when they were ambushed by Ethiopian Imperial warriors at the Battle of Massawa under the command of Menelik, the Emperor of Ethiopia.

Haile Salassie, aka *Ras tafari,* future Emperor of Ethiopia was only 4-years old at the time.

In the 1935, during the ltalio-Ethiopian War, the Ethiopian Imperial Army, now under the command of Emperor Haile Salassie, once again repelled the Italian Dictator Mussolini's "New Roman" army.

During this war, John C. Robinson, a Black man born in Mississippi, was Commander of the Imperial Ethiopian Air Corps.[63]

*　*　*　*　*

---

[63] See *the Man Called Brown Condor* by Thomas E. Simmons. Skyhorse Publications

ANOTHER WHY DIDN'T SOMEBODY TELL ME?

The Rastafarian religion (centered today in Jamaica) honors the late Emperor of Ethiopia *Haile Salassie* 1891-1975 as "King of Kings, the last descendent of wise King Solomon from The Bible and the Queen of Sheba, a great kingdom that once ruled over west Africa and Arabia.

XXXV.

Today the enemy has a name for *me---Target*.

Tomorrow I will teach him a new name for *me-Master!*

There's an old African proverb, "It's not what you call me, it's what I answer to."

In the same way you never let your opponent pick the time and place for a fight, you never let anyone pick your *name* for you.

To let an enemy *define you* allows him to *confine* you. When someone puts a label on you, they put a limit on you. Labels are what you put on a can of beans, not a man of means.

The first thing they give you when you go to prison is *a number*. Cults do the same thing, giving you some strange name not even your mama will recognize.[64]

One of the most shocking scenes in Alex Haley's 1976 book *Roots*[65]

---

[64] See "How to Start Your Own Cult" in Dr. HaHa Lung's *Lost Arts of War (Citadel Press, 2012}*
[65] The great 1977 mini-series made from the book is out on DVD.

is when the slave master whips Kunta Kinte until he's finally forced to accept his new "slave name", Toby.

*   *   *   *   *

At one time *"Mameluk"* was an Egyptian word meaning" one who is owned", in other words, *a slave*.

The Mameluks of Egypt were an elite group of *warrior* slaves especially chosen for their ferocity, trained in all the ways of warfare, and given the job of protecting their Egyptian masters from their enemies. Rich Egyptians could then send these Mameluk-slaves to fight and die in wars instead of sending their own sons.

These Mameluks were such great warriors they even defeated the great conqueror Genghis Khan in battle (something that had never been done before!), preventing a Mongol invasion of Egypt.

In 1250 AD Mameluks led by Baibars el-Rukn (aka "The Rock") revolted against their slave masters and seized power in the Egyptian capital of Cairo.

First the Mameluks established the Abbasid Dynasty that would rule Egypt for the next 300 years, and then they began conquering many of the lands around Egypt including Syria, all the way to southern Turkey and western Saudi Arabia.

From then on, in Egypt and all the lands around, when someone heard the word "Mameluk" they no longer thought "slave", they now thought "Warrior and Master"!

*   *   *   *   *

Other one-time slaves like Spartacus and Nat Turner also taught their would-be "Masters" to call them by their true names.

And who can forget the iconic photo finish of the 1964 Muhanunad Ali/ Sonny Liston fight: with Ali standing over a KO'd Liston (who defiantly refused to call the former "Cassius Marcellius Clay" by his new Muslim name)[66], yelling down at him, "What's my name! What's my name!"

* * * * *

"Great men can't be ruled."

----AynRand, *The Fountainhead, 1943*

THE TRUTH ABOUT WAR

XXXVI.

War does not feed my sons. But at least it will keep my enemy's sons from eating as well!

The following 3 Truths deal with the cruel realities of war: When to make war. How to make war. Who to make war on?

Nothing' nice.

* * * * *

---

[66] See Ali's autobiography *The Greatest: My Own Story* (1975)

Benjamin Franklin tells us that "One sword keeps another in the scabbard." In other words, if your enemies know you're going to give them "some work", they're less likely to give you any grief.

Hannibal himself used violence, but he never used "senseless" violence. Hannibal didn't do punk-assed drive-bys. He'd walk right up on your porch and ring your doorbell!

Hannibal *planned* his battles well and that's why he *won* his battles.

His attitude was always ruthless-Do whatever it takes to get the job done! --but he was never needlessly cruel nor destructive. Anytime he conquered a Roman city, he always gave the citizens a chance to join him. Many did.

Like soldiers everywhere, Hannibal never wanted to go to war.[67]

But once that first punch was thrown, he knew his job was to get the fight over with ASAP.

Put your enemy down and keep him down was -and still *is-the* Number One rule of war.

Remember how Sun Tzu advised that avoiding a fight altogether is best. But once that bell has rung, your job is to put the kind of vicious beat-down on your enemy in round one that keeps him from coming out of his comer for round two.

Malcolm said "By any means necessary."[68]

The Japanese word for this is *"Masakatsu!* ",[69] "whatever it takes".

---

[67] "1t is remarkable that soldiers by profession, men truly and unquestionably brave, seldom advise war but in case of extreme necessity." Benjamin Franklin.

[68] **"That1S our motto. We want freedom by any means necessary. We want justice by any means necessary.** *By Any Means Necessary* (Pathfinder,1970:37)

[69] **Pronounced Mass-ah-cat's-sue.**

Attila the Hun expresses this practical philosophy in his *Conqueror's Dictum:*

> "Reward all those wise enough to join you. Utterly crush all those who oppose you, and do so in so savage a way as to completely cower any and all others who might ever dream of resisting your will!"[70]

African conqueror Shaka Zulu (1787-1828) likewise taught his warriors this same "Get the job done right the first time" philosophy:

> "Follow a defeated enemy ruthlessly and put the fear of Shaka into him!"

XXXVII.

"Do not make war on women and children," they cry. Why not?

Without his woman's arms to comfort him, his ears filled with the hungry cries of his children, I have twice **discomfited my enemy!**

――――――――

"When two elephants fight, it is the grass that suffers." warns the ancient Kikuyu Kenyan African proverb, warning of the cost · your loved ones often have to pay when war comes to your front door.

Only terrorists[71] ever deliberately target women and children. Yet all too often, they get caught in the cross-fire.

―――――

[70] For all "the Answers of Attila" see *Absolute Mind Control* by Dr.Haha Lung, 2013.
[71] "Terrorist" is what the big army calls the little army.·

As hard as it is to go off to fight in a war, it's at least a little easier if you know your family is safe at home far away, or that the "civilians" in your life are off limits because your enemy respects the rule of war.

Even Omar, the most ruthless killer on *The Wire,* respected "The Game" enough to keep "civilians" out of the line of fire. That's why he went on the war-path after a couple of Avon's cowboys shot up his grandma's *hat* while he was escorting grandma to Sunday church services!

Despite Omar's other obvious short-comings, his motto was" A man has to have *a code* to live by." And, for Omar at least, that meant (I) keeping his word by always doing what he said he was going to do-which explains why everyone else was so *terrified* of him! --and (2) keeping "civilians" out of the line of fire.

Hannibal's very first Truth takes advantage of this fact by reminding his enemies what they have to Jose (what they "love the most") by going to war with him.

If a general is thinking about his home, then he's not thinking about what's going on, on the battlefield.

> "If you threaten a man's home with fire, he will rush from the· battlefield to put out that blaze."
>
> ----Spartacus

The more money a man has laying on the line, the more he's going to sweat the dice.

Sometimes we just need to remind our enemy that there's more asses on the line than just his own.

Sometimes we need to remind ourselves of this too.

*   *   *   *   *

"All men's children are precious...until *yours* hungers. Because their father looks into the face of Death, his sons will never need look into the face of Famine."

---*The Answers of Attila*

XXXVIII.

Waste is worse than war. Never burn a field that may one day feed your own sons.

———————

Ever heard "Don't cut off your nose to spite your face", "Don't rob Peter to pay Paul", or "Don't burn your bridges behind you"?

Those are all just different ways of saying "Don't destroy something you might end up needing in the future."

This includes not using people just because you can, or just because you think you don't need them anymore.

During the 1950s and 1960s "Cold War", when the two "Big Dogs" on the block kept barking at each other, but neither one of them really wanted to bite, the United States and Russia both already had nuclear weapons pointed at each other but they were still trying to develop a "neutron bomb", a bomb that would kill people but still leave buildings standing.

Seems somebody had finally figured out that it doesn't do much good to win a war unless you actually have something to show for it.

There's a big difference between "bragging rights" and "bleeding rights"!

* * * * *

"Say it loud: "I'm black and I'm proud!""

---James Brown, 1968

THE TRUTH ABOUT PEACE

XXXIX.

War should be swift, peace swifter still.

When you *have* to make war, do it quickly and do it right the first time. Likewise, when it's time to "bury the hatchet" and make peace, just do it. Study long, study wrong.

Or as Julius Caesar (63 BC-AD 14) tells it: "Well done is quickly done."

* * * * *

".... leadership is the art of accomplishing more than the science of management says it possible."

----General Colin Powell, 1995

XL.

Peace is a time for sharpening the plow.

Spy out your neighbor's ploy often.

There's a time to "turn the other cheek"...and a time to *scar* your enemy's cheek.[72]

There's a time to act "Biblical"...and a time to get "Medieva!"[73]

Any farmer who's busy plowing his field is going to be too busy to be running around making war on his neighbors.

People that never otherwise ever pick up their Bible still love quoting that verse "Beat your swords into plow" (Isaiah 2:4) when they don't feel like getting their asses kicked, or when they're stalling for time.

Those same people conveniently forget how, later on in that same Bible it says *the exact opposite,* that there's a time when it's okay to "Beat your plows into swords." (Joel3:10)

Notice how Hannibal (whose people came from the same area of the Middle East where both those Bible verses were written) warns us that, while wanting peace, we still need to keep an eye on our peaceful plowing neighbor...just in case he's trying to rock us to sleep!

＊　＊　＊　＊　＊

"Fool me once---shame on you. Fool me twice---shame **on** *me.*"

---Old Scottish saying

---

[72] "Negroes have done nothing but seen each other turn the other cheek. This generation won't do that any longer." Malcolm X (Pathfinder,1970:30)

[73] "I'm gonna get Medieval on your ass" *Pulp Fiction,* 1994. Spoken by the character Marcellus, played by Ving Rhames.

XLI.

The peace should never cost more than the war.

Ask yourself, "Is it worth it?"

Anytime you start something-whether a business or a war-you need to do what's called "cost assessment".

This isn't complicated. Simply ask yourself "Is it worth it?"

How much of your precious time and hard earned money do you have?

to put in, against how much you're going to get *out?* Will reward exceed investment?

Is the cost of setting up and running this business worth it-are you going to make?

a profit? And how long is it going to take for you to make that profit?

Is it worth spending all your hard-earned green on that shorty when everybody and their cousin knows she never puts out?

Is selling that poison on the comer really worth 10-years of your life wearing chains?

Is getting that college business degree worth missing out on all that quality time you could spend "hangin" with the "*homies*".... *Damn right it* is![74]

---

[74] "Education is our passport to the future, for tomorrow belongs to the people who prepare for it today." Malcolm
   X.
   (Pathfinder, 1970:43)

In the same way, you have to ask yourself if making peace with your enemy will benefit you in the long run, with a *lasting* peace?

Or is your enemy only *stalling* for time until he can re-arm and attack again? Is your opponent only stalling for time, till he can catch his second wind?

before jumping back in the game?

Is that sucker who owes you money only trying to slow-walk until 5-0 finally cashes in that dime he dropped on you?

Recall how after the1ˢᵗ Punic War, Rome's harsh surrender terms forced all kinds of taxes and restrictions on Carthage so that it made it almost impossible for Hannibal's people to make a living.

That's why Hannibal's warning here that anytime you make peace, you have to make sure it's a peace you can live with, a peace that, in the long run isn't going to cost you-and your sons-more than sticking to your guns and winning the war once and for all.

* * * * *

"There are some remedies worse than the disease."

---Publius Syrus, Roman Philosopher
1ˢᵗ century BC

XLII.

It is **hard to show an open hand to an enemy. Harder still to show a firm hand to a friend.**

Boss-of-all-Bosses Lucky Luciano's favorite saying was the old Sicilian proverb:

> "Do you have fifty friends? It is not enough. Do you have one enemy? It is too much!"

In the same way we need a posse to watch our back (as Hannibal pointed out in Truths XXII, XXVI, and XLII), we also need to *be* a good

``````````````````` "posse" to our friends.

You have to be a friend to have a friend.

That means having the strength to (1) never let a friend go off half-cocked, armed only with anger and false information, and (2) sometimes having to tell your friend truths they don't want to hear.

This is why Hannibal says "showing a firm hand to friend" is so hard to do. It means having the wisdom to tell the difference between "strength" and "power":

> "*Strength* is as simple as my five fingers closing to form a fist.
>
> *Power* is possessing the strength to open that fist.
>
> *Wisdom* is knowing when to open your fist and when to keep it tightly closed."
>
> ---*The Answers of Attila*

Philosopher Friedrich Nietzsche understood this:

> "This is the hardest of all: to close the open hand out of love, and keep modest as a giver."
>
> ----*Thus Spake Zarathustra, 1891*
```````````````````

That's why, still today, for men of insight and influence, this remains the rule:

> "When we are debating an issue, loyalty means giving me your honest opinion, whether you think I'll like it or not."

> ---General Colin Powell, 1995

XLIII.

So long as my right hand grips the sword and my left hand holds fast to the dagger, both remain closed to grasping friendship.

This Truth is a carry-over from the previous Truth, with Hannibal reminding us how hard it is to make peace by showing "an open hand" to an enemy.

He is also saying here that we have to keep an open mind if we ever hope to make peace with our enemies, a peace we can live with. Recall how Hannibal's people learned this the hard way when the peace treaty ending Carthage's first war with Rome shackled them with harsh restrictions they *couldn't* live with.

Given that war brings only death and destruction, you'd think people everywhere would jump at the chance to make peace with their enemies. But three things hold them back:

- First, people are *afraid* of trying to make peace with their enemies because both sides are *suspicious* that any enemy suggesting a peace treaty must be up to something (e.g. trying to draw you into a trap, or simply stalling for time till he can get some more ammunition).

Sometimes your enemy's just as tired of fighting as you are. Other times, you're right: your enemy *is* up to something.

So, it's okay to be suspicious sometimes. "Caution" and

"Paranoid" are just different sides of the same street.

Malcolm X was once accused of being a "racist", to which he responds that he wasn't "racist", just naturally- with good *cause-suspicious:*

> "I am not a racist. I don't judge a man because of his color. I get suspicious of a lot of them and cautious around them-- from experience... Not because of their color, but because of what experience has taught me concerning their overall behavior towards us."[75]

That's why Arminius (18 BC-21 AD), another enemy of Rome who followed in Hannibal's footsteps, warned:

> "Sup sparingly on suspicion. Drink deep any draught of decision."

In other words, it's okay to be careful. But once you figure out your enemy really wants peace, don't hesitate to accept it. Sure, it's hard to tell the difference sometimes, as that wise Ethiopian Aesop warned:

> "Beware lest you lose the substance by grasping at the shadow."

People are also afraid their enemy is going to get over on them, that they're going to get the worse part of the deal, and end up with "the short end of the stick".

- The second reason people are reluctant to make peace is that *change is hard.*

---

[75] *By Any Means Necessary* (Pathfinder, 1970:152)

Hannibal warned· in Truth VII against getting so "comfortable" (lazy!) that we don't even bother putting down the video game and getting up off the couch when Opportunity is pounding our door off the hinges!

Award-winning African-American author and talk-show host Tavis Smiley sums it up this way:

> "People only change because they either see the light, or else they feel the heat."

- The third reason people resist peace offers is because *they're attached to their enemies.*

That's because their enemies are often more *dependable* than their so-called friends.

The Greek philosopher Aristophanes (450-385 BC) understood this:

> "Men of sense often learn from their enemies. It is from their foes, not their friends, that cities learn the lesson of building high walls and ships of war; and this lesson saves their children, their homes, and their properties."

The Romans conquered the Greeks, so it's not surprising 200-years later that Roman philosopher Cato (95-46 BC) still agreed:

> "Some men are more beholden to their bitterest enemies than to friends who appear to be sweetness itself. The former frequently tell the truth, but the latter never."

Centuries later, wise ol' Ben Franklin would say the same thing, although with a whole lot less words:

"Love your enemies, for they shall tell you your faults." So, we're all agreed that having worthy challengers' eye-balling your championship belt *makes* you keep working out just to stay in shape and stay sharp.

Unfortunately, all too many people get "attached" to their enemies-real and imagined-because they think the bigger and badder their enemies are, the bigger and badder everybody will think *they* are.

The tougher the• crew you're going up against, the tougher *you* and your crew must be, right?

Most of the history we have on Hannibal comes from his enemies, the Romans. No sooner was Hannibal finally *confirmed* dead (and the Romans could finally breathe a sigh of relief!) than they started *praising* him for the great general he'd truly been.

Finally giving Hannibal his "props" was another way of Roman bragging, talking' smack for having "beaten" such a fierce enemy.

If still alive, Hannibal would have just smiled at this, since it's obvious he understood-and expected-this tendency in human beings. Recall Truth II: "We are made as much by our enemies as by our ambitions." while in Truth VI, Hannibal gives "thanks" for enemies who help keep him sharp.

Someone once said, "Better a true enemy than a false friend." And Machiavelli said having someone truly *fear* you (a true enemy) is more dependable than having someone *falsely love* you.

Prince Vlad Tepes couldn't agree more. There's a certain amount of certainty in having a dependable enemy who keeps you on your toes:

"An open hand, far from comforting, is an uncertainty.

Today it grips my hand in friendship, tomorrow it grasps at my purse and raises a sword against me. Give me the certainty and honesty of the fist!"[76]

*   *   *   *   *

---

[76] *Lost Arts of War* (Citadel Press,2012)

"There is no little enemy," warns Ben Franklin.

There are enough *real* enemies out there in the world that you don't have to make up fake ones.... or deliberately go out looking to make new enemies just to make yourself look bigger and badder. Afterall:

> "A little man with a big knife is still but a little man...but it's still a big knife!"[77]

> ---Prince Vlad Tepes

> "He who has a thousand friends has not a friend to spare. And he who has one enemy will meet him everywhere!"[78]

> ----Ali ibn-Abi-Ialib (602-661)
> The Hundred Sayings

XLIV.

If it began with a word, it can be ended with a word. If it began with the sword, the sword will surely end it.

In the end, you got nothing but your word. You say what you do. You do what you say. A man's word is his bond.

A man pays his bills, whether the money that's due shortly for taking care of the rug-rats, or simply an apology you owe someone for running off at the mouth.

When you're wrong, first *say* you're wrong. And then make it better

---

[77] "He who has a little knife needs a long arm." Viking_Saga *of the Vopnairthings.*
[78] aka "The Lion of God", son-ln-law of the Prophet Muhammad. 4th Caliph of Islam, assassinated 661 AD•

by *doing* better. This goes back to Sun Tzu's warning that we need to take care of little problems before they get all blown out of proportion and become big problems:

> "You pay what you owe. Or, tomorrow, you pay more.
> When has this ever ceased to be the rule?"

> ----*The Answers of Attila*

On the other hand, say you accidentally bump into someone and rightly apologize "My bad". You figure that's the end of it but the a-hole you bumped into wants to keep running his mouth about how "You should watch where you're going!", or else he's walking away but he's *mumbling* something under his breath...and it *pisses you off.*

Everybody's got a story just like this. (And it always turns out *bad!*)

In his *Art of War* Sun Tzu warns that we should always leave a man an honorable way out. That's why Sun Tzu never attacked an army who had it's back to a mountain or to the sea. With no way out, with nothing to lose, men stubbornly fight to the death.

In the same way, you never want to back a man into a comer, whether in a real fight or by boxing him in during an argument.

Like any trapped *animal,* a trapped human being can be a desperate enemy, Desperate people make "dope-fiend" moves.

So always leave a man an *honorable* way out. The Chinese call this allowing your enemy to "save face", to maintain his self-respect.

Having gotten the upper hand, having already proven your point, there's no need to punk him out just because you can.

Leave a "defeated" enemy an honorable way out and he just might thank you later.

Punk him out, and he's never going to stop trying to get back at you. Would *you?*

* * * * *

The second half of this Truth, as well as Hannibal's other thoughts on what to do when it becomes necessary-or desirable-to end a matter of "the sword" with the sword is dealt with more fully in Truths LIII, and LV through LVIII.

* * * * *

> "We all make mistakes. Sometimes we need to let those mistakes slide, you know. Sometimes we need to be bigger than the folks who don't know any better. I'm not saying we should tolerate ignorance, but maybe we should be a little more tolerant of ignorant people who step in shit and need to learn from it, or want to learn from it."
>
> •••W·hoopi Goldberg, 1997

XLV.

Shame your enemies with your mercy.

_____

Mercy isn't something you do for others. It's something you do for yourself. Despite the apparent harshness of Truth XXXVI and XXXVII, despite the fact a single word from his lips could command the death of tens of thousands, not even Hannibal's enemies could accuse Hannibal of being "without mercy".

Rather than ravage the Italian countryside, any time he conquered an Italian city, Hannibal always gave the citizens the choice to join him in his crusade against Rome. Many did choose to join him, tired of living under Roman yoke.

Even those prisoners refusing to join him were often set free...so they could spread the word[79] of Hannibal's mercy to the next town in Hannibal's path.

As a result many towns willingly threw open wide their gates and welcomed Hannibal rather than fight against him.

Leaving an honorable enemy an honorable way out, from the previous Truth, qualifies as "mercy" and, in the long run this benefits you both.

The friend you make today deprives your enemy of an ally tomorrow. This goes hand in hand with Truth XXII, where a wise general first sees to the needs of his men.

Shaka Zulu knew this.

During the Zulu's wars of conquest, the warriors of Shaka Zulu willingly sacrificed themselves for their King because they knew that Shaka would see that their families-their wives, children, and elderly parents-would be cared for:

> "Those who are not here are eating earth that we might live. Are we to forget the sorrowing mothers who bore them, and let their younger brothers and sisters go in want, because they gave their lives for Zululand? Have we not a saying that a grieving mother's heart is soothed by a stomach full of meat? Well then, let us give a double measure, with both hands, to take the taste of bitter aloes from the mouths of the sorrowing ones."

---

[79] **Today we call this "propaganda".**

--Shaka Zulu, 1819

Think of others, and others will think of you.

Foolish is the skunk who cannot smell past his own ass!

*   *   *   *   *

"While there is a lower class, I am in it. While there is
a criminal element, I am of it; while there is a soul in
prison, I am not free."

----Eugene Victor Debs, (1855-1926)

XLVI.

Mercy is the most costly of conceits...as if life and death
were truly yours to give! The power of life and death is
but on loan from The Gods. Use both wisely.

"Speak silver, reply gold," advises the ancient Swahili proverb,
meaning whatever we think we're capable of giving others, we're always
capable of giving just a little *more-101%*.

But this African proverb also tells us that we should always save a
little "mercy" for yourself: Whenever you're sure that you're at the end
of our rope, out of energy, down to your last thin dime and scraping'
the bottom of the barrel- you're still always capable of hanging on just a
little longer, capable of doing just a little *more-101%*.

Aesop says that "No Act of kindness, no matter how small, is ever
wasted," and that includes "acts of kindness" we save for ourselves.

You have to treat yourself well, because the rest of the world is too damn busy!

$$* \quad * \quad * \quad * \quad *$$

"Life is just on continuous struggle to feel good about oneself. Any time you can do anything to make anyone more pleased with him or herself, you are making life easier for that person. Conversely, if you want to make life tough for anyone, you should look for opportunities, no matter how slight or subtle, to say or do something that will make him doubt his own value."

----Fred J. Young
How to Get Rich and Stay Rich, 1992

THE TRUTH ABOUT THE GODS

XLVII.

The Gods favor those who first favor themselves,

In the 5th century BC, the famed Greek playwright Sophocles (lived 495-406 BC) wrote:

"The good befriend themselves"

Of course, Sophocles the Greek failed to mention he "borrowed" this saying from Aesop the Ethiopian slave who, a 100 years before, had written:

"The Gods help those who help themselves."

Like his enemy the Romans, like most of the peoples of his time, Hannibal's people worshiped *many* Gods.[80]

Recall that Hannibal's people originally came from the Middle East and brought with them the Gods worshiped there they called "Baals", a word meaning "Lords".

People prayed and sacrificed to these Baals for what they wanted and needed: from wives getting pregnant and having strong sons, to safe sailing (and pirating!), to their being victorious in war over their enemies. In to the Baals they brought from Middle East, Hannibal's people also worship for ages further south in Africa, Gods that took care of all the things that concerned them: from surviving natural disasters and having a good crop season, to overcoming their enemies and acquiring wealth- basically the same things that we still worry about today.

Quiet as it's kept, many of those same ancient African Gods are still worshiped today:

- *Akongo,* "The Creator", benevolent sky-god, is today still worshiped primarily in Central Africa, especially in Zaire. In Uganda, and in parts of East Africa, Akongo is called *Apap.*

- *Edeke,* the God of Disasters who is prayed to in times of famine and plague, is the brother and sometimes the rival of *Apap.*

- *Legba,* the God of Fate. Originally worshiped in parts of West Africa, especially Benin, Legba successfully crossed the Atlantic with African slaves during "The Middle Passage" to become one of the main *Mojo* Gods of Caribbean Voodoo (more properly called *Voudon).*

- *Orunmila,* the God of Destiny. Still worshiped in West Africa, especially in Nigeria. He sometimes appears as *Edshu* the Trickster to test a person's wisdom and sincerity.

---

[80] This is called "Polytheism", versus "Monotheism", meaning you worship only one God, like Jehovah or Allah.

- *Anasi* is another West African trickster who often appears in the form of a spider. In Africa a "he", Anasi also crossed the Atlantic to become "Aunt Nancy", a mysterious old Black woman who would show up unexpectedly around suppertime to test the hospitality, wit, and wisdom of slaves in the antebellum South.

- *Aje,* the always-welcome Goddess of Wealth. She is the African "Lady Luck" still widely popular in Nigeria and on other parts of West Africa.

Hannibal and his people worshiped many of these African Gods, though perhaps calling them by different names.

*   *   *   *   *

Whether Hannibal himself actually believed in any "Gods" at all we don't know for sure. He was, at the very least, respectful of the all different Gods worshiped by the warriors from many different lands who made up his army.

When reading the word "Gods" in this and the following 5 Truths just replace the word with "The Powers-that-be".

Many of the people in power-police, politicians, The Rich-do sometimes *seem* to have the power of "The Gods" over us...but only if we let them!

XLVIII.

The Gods may feast on faith...but they always wash it down with blood!

This Truth *reminds* us of two things:

First, having faith is good. Having *a plan* is better. See Truth L.

Second, you have to pay your dues. You have to pay the cost. Every culture around the world knows this.[81]

Ancient Greeks used to say "You have to pay The Ferryman!", a reference to Charon, a bony boatman in black who it was believed rowed the dearly departed across *Styx,* the River of the Dead.

The Greeks "borrowed" this idea from the Egyptian Book of the Dead, where the jackal- headed God *Anubis* guides you into the Afterlife.

Europeans still say "You gotta pay The Piper." This comes from a creepy medieval story about how a German town called Hamlin tried to cheat a conman[82] called "The Piped Piper" out of his reward after he used his magic flute to drive all the rats out of the town.

In revenge, the pissed-off Piper played another tune that hypnotized all the children into following him out of town. Neither the Piper or any of the children were ever seen again!

Down south they say, "If you want to dance, you have to pay the fiddler!", meaning you should toss some coin in that street performers' hat to show your appreciation.

And then there's the old Mafia saying:

> "Nobody rides for free, not unless you're tied up in the trunk!"

*   *   *   *   *

---

[81] Review the commentary on Truth XLIV.
[82] Never try to con a con!

"As the ground drinks freely from the torn waterskin, so too The Gods drink deeply the spilt genius[83] of the dying man.

Guard your genius well, for The Gods are a thirsty lot!"

--*The War Scroll of Spartacus*

XLIX.

We all dance for The Gods' pleasure.

Entertain them well.

There's nothing more dangerous than a bored god!

"Entertain" The Gods is Hannibal's way of saying "Come big or stay at home! Bring your A-game! Nut up or shut up!"

You either run the show or the. · show runs you. Haters and complainers only show up to slow up!

You have to actively participate in life. You can't just sit around pretending you don't care, waiting for "something" to happen, waiting for things to improve.

You're either *proactive-getting* on the scoreboard early in the game-or else you're *reactive,* always reacting to what the other players are doing, always trying to catch up.

---

[83] Back in Spartacus' day "genius" also meant your "soul" or "life force".

"If there is no struggle, there is no progress."

---Frederick Douglas (1818-1895)

"To be born, to live a short while, only to die?

Never should we imagine The Gods to be so short-sighted nor so easily entertained."

---Attila the Hun[84]

L.

Trust in The Gods....but always carry a spare sail.

A lot of Hannibal's people were sailors, so it was just common sense they'd keep extra sails on board their ships just in case they developed a tear in one of their main sails.

Without a sail, a ship is either "dead" in the water, or else it is at the mercy of any current that comes along.

People are a lot like those ships. In other words, it's better to be safe than sorry, better to carry an "extra sail" by always having a "Plan B".

The "B" in "Plan B" stands for back-up, as in you have to have *a back-up plan* ready to deal with the unexpected. Shit happens, and we don't always · smell it until we've already stepped in it!

It's okay to have "faith". But you should never act on "blind faith", faith that's too scared to ask the hard questions. That's how *cults* operate.

---

[84] See all "The Answers of Attila" in Dr. Haha Lung's *Absolute Mind Control;*

Have faith in *yourself,* in your (I) smarts and (2) in your skills.

You should also have faith in *your plans,* because you've double-checked everything that *could* go wrong and you have a "Plan B" (and maybe even a "Plan C"!) just in case anything does go wrong.

If *you* don't have faith in *your* own plans, how can you ever expect others to have faith enough in your plans to invest in them?

*   *   *   *   *

"Don't count your chickens before they're hatched."

----Aesop the Ethiopian

*   *   *   *   *

"Carpe diem!"[85]---*Horace, 65-8 BC*

"Trust in Allah, but always tie your camel."

---Arabic saying

*   *   *   *   *

"I teach my sons to trouble The Gods little, neglect them never, and trust in them.... even less!"

---Attila the Hun

---

[85] In English, "Seize the day" -

"I never walk into a room I don't know at least *two* ways out of."

----*Ronin,* 1998

*   *   *   *   *

"Always have bail money."

---50 Cent[86]

LI.

The Gods choose whom they will.... But so too do we choose our Gods!

We always have a choice.

Sure, sometimes our options *all* seem to suck! But the choice is still ours to make.

Not making a choice is almost always the *wrong* choice.

And have you ever noticed how, right after you do finally make a decision, especially a decision you've been worrying about, like maybe you've been "forced" into making a choice you really didn't want to make, that---suddenly!-- a whole bunch of other possible paths and choices occur to you?

---

[86] Quoted in The San Diego Union Tribune.

This is what Sun Tzu meant when he said: "Success has never been associated with long delays."

This doesn't mean you should jump into trouble blindly. It simply means that, if you know that sooner or later, you're going to *have to* make a choice... sooner is usually a better choice than later.

It's Universal law: Every step you take in life, no matter which direction you step, opens up new possibilities.

So as soon as you *start working in what you believe to be the right direction,* more choices will automatically present themselves to you.

The trick is to keep your options open, not to lock yourself in, to be able to change-adapt---whenever a better deal shows up.

See Truth XCVII.

*   *   *   *   *

"I want to be anywhere in the world that I'm needed."

---Dennis Rodman (after being criticized for
visiting North Korea in March, 2013)[87]

LII.

The pull of the current, will and warriorhood, and the whim of The Gods: These three determine a man's fate.

---

[87] The Week 3/22/13.

This Truth follows up on the previous Truth by telling us how broad or narrow the path we walk in life, how many numbers of choices we have in life J will depend on how well we balance 3 factors:

- *The pull of the current:* Another Hannibal reference to sailing that's really *not* about sailing.

"Current" here means how much you know about your environment (where you live, where you work, etc.), and how well you're tuned in to the feelings and attitudes of the people around you.

What works fine in one place and time might not work at all in another time or place. What plays in Harlem might not play in Houston or in Honolulu.

We all talk different---choosing different words, using our "inside voice" more--when talking to our Grams than we do when kickin' it with the fellas down at the B-ball park.

The same goes for when we're looking to get hired somewhere. We dress the part, dressing differently if we're trying to get hired by Walmart than by John Gotti.

We walk the walk, and talk the talk-whatever walk and whatever talk we think is (I) going to get us in the door, and (2) get us the job.

There's nothing wrong with changing up--and *stepping up! ---your* game, to fit time and place. Just the opposite: Being able to *adapt* means you're *smart* enough to know the difference between a boardroom and a barroom.

Ocean currents pull and push ships one way or the other. So, Hannibal's "current" is also talking about the things and people that pull you here and push you there: your desires, drives, and dreams:

> "Your dreams give you license to see beyond your circumstances to your *possibilities.*"

> ---Isaiah Thomas

It's important you *understand-admit to--your* desires, drives, and dreams before your enemy discovers them and finds a way to use them against you.

- *Will & Warriorhood:* "Will"=focus (knowing what you want) + determination (sticking to it until you get what you want).

"Warriorhood" is focus+ determination + honor (doing what you say you're going to do).

- *The Whim of the Gods* means that, no matter how well you map out your strategy, there's always going to be something (or someone) you *didn't* count on that comes along determined to throw "shit" in the game and mess up your plans.

What can you do about this? *Plan better.* And always have a "Plan B".

Most time we can't even tell what other *people* are thinking. Let alone "The Gods"!

Don't forget: When you read "The Gods", just think ·The Powers-that-be", as in anyone who *thinks* they hold power over you.

When it comes to depending on the "whim" of The Gods (or "The Powers-that-be"), Hannibal would have agreed with Chinese philosopher Ch'en Tu-hsiu, (1879-1942):

> "Man's happiness in life is the result of man's own effort and is neither the gift of God nor a spontaneous natural product."

∗ ∗ ∗ ∗ ∗

Of these three-the pulls of the current; will & warriorhood; and the whim of The Gods, you can only control your own will and your own warriorhood.

Together your "will" and your "warriorhood" add up to your *fate*.

*   *   *   *   *

When someone's car breaks down out on the highway they call "Triple A"[88]

In order to keep moving full-speed down the road of life, you use "The 4 A's":

- *Anticipating:* It's just like chess; Figuring out how your enemy is going to move before he even knows himself.

By deliberately limiting his options-boxing him in, removing his pieces from the board-you limit the number of moves open to him, leaving him only a limited number of ways he can respond to your moves. Now you got him on the run, playing a defensive game.

- *Adapting:* The greatest of Greek philosophers, Socrates, advised his students to "Study to be what you wish to seem."

In other words, find yourself a "role model", someone who knows something you don't, a skill you want to learn. Shut up long enough to learn that skill. Thank your teacher. And then move on to your *next* role model.

The skills of yesterday might not get you through tomorrow. Maybe they will, maybe they won't. Either way, keep learning new skills. You never know what might come in handy.

- *Achieving:* It's okay to pat yourself on the back for a hard-fought victory. And it's okay to pay yourself first, Afterall you earned it.

Be a "gracious" winner.... but always be an *alert* winner.

---

[88] **The American Automotive Association.**

- *Advancing:* While you're taking your bows and accepting your award, part of you should already be planning your *next* victory.

It's Aesop the Ethiopian's "Tortoise and the Hare" lesson again: While you're busy doing your end-zone dance and bragging about your *last* victory, the guy you just beat isn't taking a day off, he's already heading back to the gym.

While you're busy partying, he's busy planning his *next* bid for your championship belt. They say "There's no rest for the wicked" and this includes generals, businessmen, sports stars, and even entertainers.

Yesterdays' awards and victories, whether a record-making military victory or business deal; a Guinness Book of World Records sports accomplishment; or a #I selling hip-hop record...that was *yesterday.*

"Stay hungry" if you want to keep your belly full. There'll be time enough to rest when you're *dead!*[89]

*   *   *   *   *

"The real measure of success is your ability to keep growing by seeking new challenges, looking for new opportunities, and setting even higher and more ambitious goals while making sure you measure your progress against your ultimate, long term, most deeply-rooted-goals.... You climb one mountain and then you look for a higher one.

---Isaiah Thomas

---

[89] Or when all your *enemies* are dead!

THE TRUTH ABOUT REVENGE

LIII.

The wine of a true friend is fine indeed. But some thirsts can only be satisfied by the blood of a foe!

———————————

The Mafia word for it is *vendetta.*

Hillbillies call it "feudin'".

And out there on those mean streets everybody already knows, or learns *fast,* that "Payback's a bitch!"[90]

Taking revenge against one's enemies was an accepted and *expected* (and therefore, planned for!) practice in Hannibal's day.

Of course, in our modem "politically correct" age we're not supposed to think about getting "revenge" against someone who's done us dirty.

Sure, you're right...That's why most of these 50 United States still have the death penalty--"The Edison Medicine", "Suckin" the Pipe"; or "The Gurney Journey". And that's why everyone was clapping so hard when we heard Osama bin Laden was finally sleeping with the fishes!

One man's "revenge" is another man's "justice".

> "Now, if it is deemed necessary that I should forfeit my life for the furtherance of the ends of justice, and mingle my blood further with the blood of my children, and with the blood of millions in this slave country, whose

---

[90] "Violence is as American as cherry pie." (Black Power activist H. Rap Brown)

rights are disregarded by wicked, cruel, and unjust enactments. I submit: so, let it be done!"

----John Brown's death speech, 1859

So, if the word "revenge" bothers you, call it 'justice", or simply think of it as "balancing the books" instead.

"Two wrongs don't make a right...But it damn sure makes it even!"

---Sister Souljah

Even your Auntie's Holy Bible is crammed full of "An eye for an eye" revenge stories and sayings

Check out the Second Book of Kings, chapter 9, where the Hebrew warrior Jehu gets his revenge by overthrowing evil King Joram and by then killing Joram's equally-evil whore-Queen, Jezebel[91]

Or how about in the Bible book *The Wisdom of Jesus Son of Sirak* (written about 180 BC) where we're taught the eight tools we can use for revenge:

"Fire and hail and famine and pestilence, all these have been created for vengeance; the teeth of wild beasts, and scorpions and vipers, and the sword that punishes the ungodly with destruction...."(39:29-30)

Jesus Son of Sirak goes on to remind us how a good son is expected to avenge any wrongs done his dead father:

---

[91] Cutthroat stories like this one are why they don't like you reading all the good sex and violence in the *Old* Testament.
Right, because You might get too many ideas!

"The father may die, and yet he is not dead, for he has left behind him one like himself....an avenger against his enemies, and one to repay the kindness of his friends."[92]

And then there's always The Book of Revelation---when God rains down some serious vengeance---justice---on *all* his enemies.

The Muslim Holy Qur'an likewise gives us the greenlight for revenge:

"If any one transgresses against you, transgress you likewise against him." (Sura 2:194)

"Life for life, eye for eye, nose for nose, ear for ear, tooth for tooth, and wounds equal for equal." (Sura 5:45)

"The recompense for an injury is an injury equal thereto." (Sura 42:40)

Evidently, not only is one man's "revenge" another man's ') justice", one man's "punishment" can also be another man's "revenge".

LIV.

The nearer the blood, the more it burns.

Blood always tells, but you may not like its tales.

This Truth talks about two different types of" revenge":

---

[92] "That's why they took those "Apocraphal" books out of the original Bible. Right, because you might get too many ideas!

(I) Our taking revenge against someone for something they've done to our family and friends-for committing an offense against our "blood".

"The nearer the blood, the more it bums." means the· closer we are to someone, the more it bothers us (" bums us") when we see somebody messing with them.

(2) "The nearer the blood" also refers to when we realize we've been sold-out by someone close to us.

Betrayal "bums" too, and that's why we "may not like its tales". Yeah, the way Fredo betrayed Michael in *The Godfather.*

In other words, the last thing in the world we want to hear is that someone close to us has sold us out either deliberately or, often accidentally.

Romulus, the founder of Rome, was betrayed by his brother Remus. Romulus killed him.

At the battle of Zama, Hannibal was betrayed by his ally and "blood brother" Masinissa, the Prince of Numidia.[93]

Prince Vlad Tepes was betrayed by his brother Radu, who converted to Islam and became the minion (lover) of the Turkish Sultan who was holding the boy's hostage. Radu later fought on the side of Muslims invading Vlad's kingdom.[94]

Attila the Hun slew his brother Bieda after realizing his brother cared more for Roman gold than for Hun steel and honor.

In 1828 African conqueror Shaka Zulu was assassinated by 2 of his scheming step-brothers.

---

[93] The African Kingdom just south of Carthage. See Truth LXXXI.
[94] "Turn your back on your blood and the world turns its back on you." --Vlad Tepes, Certainty LXV. For all 72 of Prince Vlad's "Certainties" see *Lost Arts of War* (Citadel, 2012).

On the other hand, Joseph in the book of Genesis was thrown into slavery by his brothers, but chose *not* to take any revenge on them later when he had become a high-n-mighty prince in Egypt.

> "You have seen how a man was made a slave; you shall see how a slave was made a man."
>
> ----Frederick Douglas, 1845

LV.

Revenge should wait until both your sword and your wits have been sharpened.

———————————

Here "sword" means the *resources* you have available.

"Wit" means *intelligence,* both the kind you're born with and the kind of intelligence ("intel") you gather by paying attention and by paying spies.

Right tools. Right timing.

Number one best revenge story ever? *The Count of Monte Cristo,* written by a Black Frenchman named Alexandre Dumas in 1845.

In this story, an illiterate sailor named Edmond Dantes from the French port of Marseilles gets set up by four haters and ends up sent to prison for life for a crime he didn't commit.

Dantes spends the next 15-years in prison, during which time he meets a former-priest who's also a prisoner who helps Dantes educate himself, turning an illiterate sailor into an educated gentleman.

When they become friends, the priest offers to share a pirate treasure hidden on the deserted island of Monte Cristo with Dantes once they escape. The priest dies soon after but Dantes succeeds in escaping and finding the treasure.

Now rich, disguised as the mysterious "Count on Monte Cristo" Dantes returns to Marseilles where he successfully plots revenge of the four haters who sent him to prison.

Final body count: two of his haters wind up dead, one loses his fortune and has his reputation ruined, and one is driven insane!

Dumas' *the Count of Monte Cristo* has been made into a movie several times. The book also inspired the 1994 movie *The Shawshank Redemption,* written by Stephen King and starring Tim Robbins and Morgan Freeman. The book *The Count of Monte Cristo* is even mentioned in the movie when some hillbilly mispronounces Alexandre Dumas' name. "Dumb-ass". It's correctly pronounced "DUE-MA".

LVI.

Revenge demands a steady hand and a steadier eye

When Hannibal says "steady" hear "sticking to it", doing what you said you were going to do.

When you read "steady hand" think *determination*

"Steadier eye", that means having *focus* (another word for "concentration") and *patience* (another word for not getting in so much of a hurry that you make stupid mistakes).

The really important things in life, like revenge, don't usually give you a second chance.

Again, this means gathering "Intelligence" of both kinds, the kind the Good Lord gave you and the kind you find and figure out on your own.

*   *   *   *   *

"I do not feel sorry for what I have done. God will judge my acts."

---Nat Turner, at his trial.

*   *   *   *   *

"Forgiveness is between them and God....My job is to arrange the meeting."

----Denzel Washington, *Man on Fire,2004*

LVII.

Revenge demands a long blade....and a longer memory.

In this Truth Hannibal tells us the two things we definitely have to have if we're going to succeed in doing *anything,* especially when trying to "balance" wrongs done us.

- A "long blade" means having the *resources* to do what we need to do to accomplish our goal. How much gas-money you going to need to get where you're trying to get to?

- A "longer memory" again teaches *patience*, the greatest skill you can ever have, the skill without which it's impossible to learu all the other skills.

Remember: "Revenge is a dish best eaten cold." Have the patience to let it cool, or else you might end up burning your own tongue.

"A longer memory" is also Hannibal's way of warning us that, in the same way *you* would never forget a wrong done to you or to one of your friends or family, *your enemy* might be thinking the same way.

So, don't make enemies if you don't have to.

The old Chinese warns: "Never strike a king unless you're sure you can kill him." Tipping your hand, making your move before you're ready and failing-whether when making a business deal, launching a new product linc, or getting revenge--only invites your enemies to take revenge against you, and maybe against your friends and family.

Suddenly the hunter has become the hunted! Watch your back.

* * * * *

In the end, there's an old saying that "The best revenge is doing well."

This means is that nothing pisses your haters off more than seeing you *live* the good life.

* * * * *

"You're either part of the solution or part of the problem."

----Eldridge Cleaver, Black Panther leader, 1964

* * * * *

"Of all that is written, I love only what a person hath written with his blood."

----Friedrich Nietzsche,
German Philosopher 1844-1900

"If your actions are upright and benevolent, be assured they will augment your power and happiness."

---Kurush, aka "Cyrus the Great",
King of Persia 590-529 BC

LVIII.

Revenge, like fine wine and royal blood, takes time to ferment properly.

All successful revenge stories have two things in common: *patience* and a *determination to act* no matter what the cost,

While never openly preaching "revenge", Malcolm X was adamant that final victory must be obtained "By any means necessary!"

That's why Malcolm was never prejudice when it came to traveling far and wide to gather up whatever intelligence---knowledge and skills-he needed to carry him one step closer to his goal. It didn't matter what the source of that "intelligence" was.

As a result, Malcolm could argue history and philosophy and strategy with the best of them, and he didn't mind quoting from the best of them, even from Shakespeare:

"I read once, passingly, about a man named Shakespeare-I only read about him passingly, but I remember one thing he wrote that kind of moved me. He put it in the mouth of Hamlet, I think it was, who said, "To be or not to be"--he was in doubt about something--"whether to suffer the slings and arrows of outrageous fortune"--moderation---"or to take up arms against a sea of troubles, and by opposing, end them." And I go for that. If you take up arms you'll end it. But if you sit around and wait for the one who's in power to make up his mind that he should end it, you'll be waiting a long time."

---Malcolm X, 1964[95]

Hamlet, written in 1604, is considered Shakespeare's greatest play, and is all about *revenge*.

Young Prince Hamlet returns home to Denmark from school in Germany to find that his father the King has secretly been murdered by his own brother-Hamlet's uncle-who is now the King.

Hamlet plots his revenge while pretending to be crazy (in order to rock his evil uncle to sleep).

When the evil King finally realizes Hamlet isn't really crazy and is on to him, he sends two hit-men to kill Hamlet.

In the end, Hamlet outwits the would-be assassins and ultimately succeeds in killing the King...but Hamlet dies in the process.

*　*　*　*　*

---

[95] *By Any Means Necessary,* (Pathfinder, 1970:182)

"But I ain't never crossed a man that didn't deserve it. Me be treated like a punk? You know that's unheard of!"

---*Gangsta's Paradise*

THE TRUTH ABOUT HONOR

LIX.

Duty flows out from my heart. Obligation pours into my ear!

Hannibal's next 5 Truths all deal with "Honor", a word that means different things to different people, depending on their perspective. Truth LXXXII explains "perspective" well.

"Honor" is simply:

(1) You doing what you *say* you're going to do.

(2) You doing what you're *supposed* to be doing, what you signed up to do. That's called doing your "duty".

Hannibal never let a rival general pick the time or place of a battle they were going to fight.

Never let other people pick your battles for you. Never let others pick your friends for you.

In the same way, don't let someone else tell you what your "duty" is.

People try to "obligate" us all the time. They try to put tax on us that we don't really owe[96] or else try to "guilt" us into doing something for them (usually by claiming to have done a similar favor for us already).

Don't fall for it.

We'll say again: In the, end, all you have is *your word*.

Keeping your word works for you two ways.

- First, saying what you mean and doing what you say earns you *a reputation* for being dependable, this makes people trust you.

When people know they can trust you to do your best to keep your promises to them, they'll do all they can to help you do whatever you're trying to do.

When an army knows they can trust their general, to keep his word, they'll follow him into Hell!

- Keeping your word also makes untrustworthy people *fear* getting in your way or otherwise interfering with your plans because, when you tell them point-blank that there's a *price* to be paid for crossing you, they know to take you at your word.

That's why reputation spills less blood. Review Truth XXIX.

*   *   *   *   *

"Let me explain to you. I'm in charge and you ain't. That's what the troops needed to hear."

----General Colin Powell, 1993

---

[96] Mafia loanshark types call this kind of tax on real or imagined services performed for others, and/or interest on money loaned, *"The Vig"*.

LX.

He who fights for blood soon finds it dripping from his own heart.

He who fights for glory never lives long enough to hear the victory songs.

He who fights for gold is already blinded by the glitter and the glare of his own greed, all too soon led astray by all things shiny.

He who fights for sport seldom finds The Gods in a sporting mood.

He who fights for love must leave the one he loves the most behind so he can dance with the one he hates the most. But he who fights for honor cannot be led astray.

This Truth gives us what has been called "Hannibal's Six Movers of Men"[97] what he saw as the six attitudes and goals that motivate people: Blood; Glory; Gold; Sport; Love; and, most importantly, Honor.

Twenty-two hundred years before *Psychology* was recognized as a "science", Hannibal was already pretty good at "sizing up" potential warriors for his army, and figuring out the motivations of his current and future enemies.

He had to be.

---

[97] *Mind Warrior: Strategies for Total Mental Domination* by Dr. Haha Lung and Christopher B. Prowant. Citadel/ Kensington Books, 2010.

Allowing even one *coward* or *traitor* to join his crew, thinking someone was a friend when they were really a foe with a good cover game, spelled the difference between life and death back in Hannibal's day.

Right. Same thing *today*.

Let the wrong wire-for-hire climb into your car and you and the rest of your true crew are in for a world of hurt!

We need to know what makes people tick before we can either wind them up.... or else stop their clock!

Hannibal goes more into this with Truths LXIV through LXXIII on "The Truth about the Nature of People".

LXI.

Skin cut a thousand times eventually heals. Honor wounded but once never heals.

The difference between an amateur and a professional is that a professional knows when to walk away.

Remember that scene in *The Outlaw Josey Wales* (1976) where a bounty-hunter stands ready to draw his pistol on Clint Eastwood's character:

> "We don't have to do this," Josey Wales calmly tells the man. "A man's gotta make a living," the bounty-hunter shrugs. "Dyin' ain't much of a livin'," Josey tells him coldly. Hesitating for a moment, the man turns and walks away. Survivor of 5 years of civil war and a hundred personal gunfights, Josey Wales just waits,

knowing what's coming. A minute later, the bounty-hunter returns.

"I had to come back," he tells Josey.

"I know," Josey sighs.

Josey Wales kills the bounty-hunter before the man can clear leather.

It's just a movie. But was it the man's greed for the reward being offered for Josey Wales' head or the man's *pride and honor* that just wouldn't let him walk away?

We'll never know. After all, it's just a movie.

⋆ ⋆ ⋆ ⋆ ⋆

Sometimes it's hard to just "Forgive and forget". Just ask Osama bin Laden.

Sometimes we hold on to our hatin' because it's easier to keep hating our enemy than it is to make peace with them. Remember Truth XLIII?

Or else we stubbornly refuse to admit when we've fucked up because of our anger, greed, or out of a sense of honor.... basically, all the six things Hannibal mentioned in the previous Truth, *plus fear.*

Man up. Apologize. Move on:

"Don't stay attached to what's happened. Instead,

> eliminate that fear by letting go of your past and focusing on what needs to be done now. Trust me, it actually feels good to admit you've been wrong about something. Sitting in front of a group on people and saying, "Sorry, but I fucked up," is surprisingly easy (though you definitely

don't want to get into a habit of doing it). Admitting that you were wrong isn't only easy, it's actually fun. It dissolves all the tension and lets you focus on your next move. What's hard is setting in front of those same people and trying to convince them that you didn't fuck up when you and they both know that you did."

---Russell Simmons, 2007

LXII.

War always begins with deceit. This is why war is always the final recourse of an honorable man.

As every strategist from SW1 Tzu to Muhammad to 50-Cent has pointed out:

War is deception.

For the rest of the time, however, it's always better to deal straight up with a person then to go behind their back.

If nothing else, that just means less pissed off people you have to keep track of!

Dealing honestly with people increases your street-cred, giving you a reputation as someone who can be trusted.

None of us likes having to deal with a lying, conniving sleeze-ball who's always trying to screw us over or else nickel and dime us to death.

Sure, sometimes we're forced to deal *with-confront--deceitful* people.

But that doesn't mean we have to *like* dealing with those kind of boss-cross stab-you- in-the-back Mfers!

The less you have to deal with lowlifes.... the better your chances of living the high life.

Does any of the following sound familiar:

- Like attracts like.

- What goes around, comes around.

- Lie down with dogs, get up with fleas.

- Or how about The Bible's "Whatsoever a man soweth, so shall he reap." In other words, Payback's a bitch...and her name is *Karma!*

You really are known by the company, clique, and crew you keep.

And while you may for the most part be a God-fearing' honest person, if you're always seen hanging' with a bunch of deceitful double-crossing' dogs, sooner or later people are going to think you got fleas too, that you're also a deceitful double-crossing' dog. As a result, honest folk are going to naturally shy away from doing business with you.

"The rich rob the poor and the poor rob one another."

---Isabella Van Wagener
(aka Sojourner Truth, 1787-1883)

LXIII.

War always ends in desperation and death...and the death of honor is the most tragic of these.

A continuation of the previous Truth.

Get caught telling a lie once, and you're going to be branded a liar for life. Yeah, life's hard like that.

Admit it: You catch your baby's mama or one of your home-boys in a lie and, though you *say* you forgive them, from then on, every time they tell you something you're always going to be wondering "Are they lying to me *again?*"

Hanging' with a bunch of deceitful lying-ass double-crossers makes it all too easy for us to fall into a habit of backstabbing behavior ourselves, tempting us to compromise our principles and betray our personal sense of honor just to keep up with *their* bullshit!

Before we know it, our name starts to taste like shit in honest folks' mouths.

*   *   *   *   *

Yeah, yeah, I know. Right about now you're thinking, "I don't give a shit what people think of me!"

Well, guess what, because of the way you're backstabbing people like you think The Spine Store is going to go out of business sometime soon, people are now thinking *your little brother and little sister* are up to no-good just like their *big brother.*

Every time you go wallowing in the gutter, you're taking your mama, your grandma, little brother and little sister, your baby's mama and your babies, all the friends and family you *claim* you love, down into that gutter with you.

That means 5-0's going to be eyeballing' your little brother and your little sister even more, thinking' they must be up to no good too...just like their big brother.

And the reason your mama didn't get that call back from that place where she was trying to get that job, she wanted so bad? Because...just look at how her *son* turned out. If she can't raise her own children, how's she going to help me run my business better?

Just keeping' it real. Life's hard to begin with. But it's a whole lot harder for a man without *honor* and other higher virtues:

> "Honesty, for example, is a highly regarded value among most cultures. So is courage. So are self-reliance, loyalty, kindness, and service to others. The values that you choose to live by are personal. They may change radically as your life and circumstances change, but hopefully, you will establish a strong core of values early in life and follow them. Without certain values as guidelines, you may feel as if you are drifting along, just taking life as it comes. A strong set of values is vital to your success and to your survival in a competitive world. With them as your foundation, you can more easily act based *on* what you *believe in,* rather than based on what is happening to you. Values give you power to respond to challenges thoughtfully rather than emotionally.
>
> -----Isaiah Thomas, 2001

*　*　*　*　*

"A good reputation is more valuable than money."

----Publius Syrus, 1" century
Roman Philosopher

THE TRUTH ABOUT THE NATURE OF PEOPLE

LXIV.

Employ men according to their humors, deploy men according to their fevers.

Back in Hannibal's day "humors" had nothing to do with being funny, instead the word meant "emotions" and "attitudes".

Prince Vlad Tepes, the real "Dracula", said it this way:

"What a man loves, defines him. What a man hates, refines him. Both, in tum, confine him."[98]

So, this Truth is really all about

(1) Learning to size people up (using what Hannibal taught us in Truth IV about "The 4 Pillars" that hold up a man's house, and Truth LX, where we learned the "6 Movers of Men").

(2) Putting people to work doing what they're best suited to do. Putting the right person in the right place at the right time is how a general wins battles.

*   *   *   *   *

---

[98] You'll find all 72 of Dracula's "Certainties" in Lung's Lost *Art War* (Citadel Press, 2012)

"Wars may be fought with weapons, but they are won by men."

-----General George S. Patton 1885-1945

* * * * *

"Weapons are an important factor in war, but not the decisive one; it is man and not materials that count."

---Mao Tse-Tung, 1893-1976[99]

LXV.

The most treacherous of beasts wears its fur on the inside.

Only one beast wears its fur on the "inside"...the human beast!

By "fur" Hannibal means those things *and people-family* and friends-we keep close to our heart, those things and people that give us hope and help keep us warm in an all-too-often cold, cruel world.

Wearing your "fur on the inside" can also mean our hidden hates and darker desires we don't let others see, for example, our prejudices, and plans of payback.

Polite society and political correctness often demand that we wear our "fur" on the inside--keeping our desires and hates, fears and prejudices to ourselves.

-----

[99] The guerrilla Commander who became ruler of China. Mike Tyson has an inspirational tattoo of Mao's face on his bicep.

Rather than tell-and then *show! --someone* what you really think of them, and accidentally "offend" someone, you're expected to "Bite your tongue" and "Turn the other cheek".

Be careful you don't "turn the other cheek" so much that you start looking down on your own ass!

*　　*　　*　　*　　*

Can a leopard really change his spots? Can people ever really change? "Should someone tell you that a mountain has moved from this place to that, you are free to believe this. But i.;anyone tells you tbat a man has changed his character, believe it not."

----Muhammad

LXVI.

The barking of beasts is a blessed thing...it warns of their approach. Do not fear the noise, fear the silence.

There's a time to shut up, and there's a time to nut up, and often that means speaking up--no matter the price to be paid:

"I'd rather speak out about something I believe in and be broke than stay silent and get paid."

----Russell Simmons, 2007

There's a time to dribble...and a time to break for the basket. If you can't tell the difference, you got no business trying' to hold court.

What's that the NBA pros say about showboating' rookies who "Talk slick, but can't stick no brick!"

On the other hand, they're *too quiet,* that means they're up to something!

> "I do not fear the grumbling of the people...I fear their silence."
>
> ---Prince Vlad Tepes

Remember Truth XIII?

LXVII.

Back-slapping in fat times, back-stabbing in lean. In lean times, one piece of meat is just as good as another.

My enemy's heart is just meat!

Attila the Hun warned that "The sharpest spear point does not benefit from a crooked shaft."

In other words, surrounding yourself with a bunch of suckers isn't going to help your cause much.

It's not the enemies that kick you when you're down you need to worry about.

It's your so-called friends who kick you to the curb at the first sign of trouble.

Donald Trump and Russell Simmons are friends for life today because, believe it or not, there was a time back-in-the-day when "The Donald" was neck-deep in debt and Russell Simmons was the only one who stepped up to help his friend get back right.

* * * * *

"Prosperity makes friends, adversity tries them."

---Publius Syrus
1st century BC Roman philosopher

See Truth LXX.

LXVIII.

An enemy may blacken your face with blows, but only you can blacken your own heart.

Your "principles" are what makes you, *you.*

Your "principles" are:

- What you stand for (e.g. what you believe in);

- What you *can't stand* (e.g. liars, betrayers); and

- What you *won't* put up with (e.g. your personal line of *honor* only the foolish and the suicidal dare to cross!).

It's not about being stubborn, it's about being consistent, about saying what you mean, and doing what you say.

Right, we're back on *that* again.

Keep your word and don't break bread with those who don't keep their word. Don't compromise your principles, and never tolerate someone else trifling with, tampering with, testing, or otherwise trying to compromise your principles.

Don't let some sucker pull you over to his side of the street. Stand *tough* or fall rough.

Take this Truth and Truth LXIII to heart.

In his 2009 autobiography *Uncommon*[100] Tony Dungy, who played in the NFL for three years before becoming the first African-American coach to win a Super Bowl (in 2007), describes "toughness" like this:

> "Toughness is shown in how you respond to adversity. Can you respond without losing your footing and your direction? If so, that shows that you're tough. Life is messy. We don't always get a happy ending, and sometimes the middle isn't so happy either. You never really know how tough people are until they encounter the rough spots. We're all tough when things are going our way. We're all tough when we're getting the breaks."[101]

LXIX.

Trust the heart before you trust the skin.

His skin is **white but his heart is black.**

His skin is **black but his heart is white.**

All blood runs red.

———————————

One of the most kick-ass martial arts fighting systems today is the Israeli *Krav Maga.*

———————————

[100] **"Success is uncommon, therefore not enjoyed by common man." Tony Dungy, Ibid.**
[101] *Uncommon by* Tony Dungy with Nathan Whitaker. Tyndale, 2009:139

But rather than being an ancient fighting system like the Asian arts of *Kung Fu*[102] and *Karate,* Krav Maga is a 20th century *mixture* taking the best self-defense (and killing!) techniques from *all* martial arts styles.

Hannibal's army was like that, made up of the best fighters from many different nations and peoples.

Hannibal's enemies, the Romans, also understood this idea. Their symbol was called fasces, *a* bundle of sticks tied together.

By themselves, each one of these sticks could easily be broken but, when bundled together, the bunch couldn't be broken.

Wallace Deen Muhammad[103] put it this way:

"Honey comes from many differently-colored flowers."

$$* \quad * \quad * \quad * \quad *$$

The lesson here is that we should never turn down an idea, a new tool (or weapon), or any offer of help when we're in need just because it comes from a stranger.....or the other side of the tracks:

- That new idea might just be your *first* million waiting to happen.

- That new tool (or weapon) might just be what you need to fix whatever's broken (or whatever it is that *needs breaking).*

- That stranger might just be a friend waiting to happen.

Of course, it goes without saying that you can't afford to be a sucker about every open hand begging you for a dime.

---

102 More properly called *Wu-shu.*
103 Son of Elijah Muhammad, founder of The Nation of Islam.

Use your common sense-and that means use your eyes and ears. And trust your gut.

Just because someone looks like you, doesn't mean they *think* like you.

*   *   *   *   *

> "The government will not save you. The black leadership will not save you. You're the only one who can make the difference. Whatever your dream is, go for it."

----Earvin "Magic" Johnson, 1992

LXX.

Failure boasts few friends.

There are no feasts at Failure's table, his sons fallen to the sword and to slavers.

The *Samurai* warriors of Japan have a shout: "Nine times down, ten times up!", meaning no matter how many times you get knocked down, you have to keep getting back up.

When African-American "Samurai" and decorated Gulf War veteran General Colin Powell was asked to reveal his "secret" of success, he generously took the time to give us the following five steps to success:

> "There are no secrets to success; don't waste time looking for them...Success is the result of perfection, hard work, learning from failure, loyalty to those for

whom you work, and persistence. You must be ready for opportunity when it comes."[104]

Did you catch that. step about "learning from failure"?

Nine times down. Ten times up.

That old cliché' still holds water: "Winners never quit and quitters never win." Entrepreneur Russell Simmons learned a lot in school, but, lucky for him, he never learned to spell "quitter":

> "Some people who are the least talented, but are the harder workers and more resilient, end up with the most success. I ought to know, because I'm definitely one of them. The reason most people fail to reach the finish line is because they confuse a setback with a failure...You have to see every failure as a test of your resilience. Just like you must accept that the universe is always going to say no at first when you come up with a new idea. That's why your job is to always make the universe say yes."

> (Ibid. 2007)

Another successful African-American TV personality Tavis Smiley is likewise a "bad speller":

> "Rejection is re-direction." (Smiley, 2011)

And, of course, Russell's friend Donald Trump shares the same attitude. Says "The Donald":

> "If there is a concrete wall in front of you, you have to go through it. You can never, ever give up or even think in terms of giving up."

---

[104] *The Washington Post* 1.15.89.

Your "fair-weather friends" from Truth LXVII? They not only know all-too well how to spell "quitter"...they've all got matching tattoos of it!

LXXI.

The emotions of men shift as surely as the wind and are as unsteady as the shifting sands.

If human beings were predictable, then they wouldn't be human beings.

Unlike the wind, which comes and goes from only from dependable directions, a person's emotions are liable to come from anywhere at any time, appearing without warning, and disappearing just as mysteriously.

Like most men of wisdom, Aesop didn't have much use for liars and for immature people whose emotions and attitudes and honesty was less dependable than the wind:

> "I have nought to do with men who can blow hot and cold with the same breath."

Inspired by the wisdom of" The Ethiop", Greek philosopher Horace (65-8 BC) would later come to the• conclusion that "People are a many-headed beast!", his way of pointing out that human beings are the most unpredictable of animals.

There's a big difference between being "predictable"--a bad thing--and being "dependable"--a good thing.

If you're too predictable, people will take advantage of you.

If you're not dependable...people will stop depending on you and they will soon go elsewhere looking for a leader, a friend, a lover they *can* depend on.

*   *   *   *   *

"If you know how they tick, you can make them emotional."

---50-Cent[105]

*　*　*　*　*

"Never underestimate the predictability of stupidity."

----*Snatch*, 2000

LXXII.

Beware calling another man "genius." A tree always looks tallest when surrounded by shrub.

The "Godfather of Hip-Hop" Russell Simmons might be a billionaire entrepreneur now-founder of Def Jam Records, Phat Farm, the Def Comedy Jam and all that-but there was a time when he was still hustling those mean streets just to stay alive. So, nobody can say he's not seen life from two very *different perspective-looking* up from the street until he could look down from the penthouse.

But just because he can now look out his penthouse window down onto those mean streets, that doesn't mean he looks "down" on the rest of us who are still hustling those mean streets to make ends meet.

Just the opposite.

---

[105] *Wired* March, 2013:64

Today Russell Simmons devotes much of his time and considerable fortune to helping other up-n-comers to see the world from a more realistic, more positive perspective.

In his 2007 *Do You! 12 Laws to Access the Power in YOU to Achieve Happiness and Success.*[106] he tells us:

> "If you see the world as a happy, loving place, then that's where you're going to live. But if you see the world as a messed up, negative and dangerous place, then that will be your reality."

That's called *"perspective"*, and perspective simply means how we see ourselves and others. The more *realistic* our perspective, the• better our chances for success.

Ever heard the old *African* story about the three blind men who all touched an elephant for the first time?

- The first blind man touched only the tail, so he thought an elephant was like *a snake.*

- The second blind man touched only the elephant's trunk, so he was convinced an elephant was like *a tree.*

- The third blind man was just as certain that an elephant was like *a wall,* since he'd only run his hand along the side of the elephant.

And remember Edshu, the West African Trickster-God mentioned in Truth XLVII? The Yoruba people of Nigeria are always on the look-out because they know Edshu gets his rocks off by making stupid people argue and fight with one another after *he* stirs up shit between them.

You see when Edshu walks around in the world he looks like a normal person, maybe even somebody you know, but he always wears this tricky hat that's colored a different color on all four sides: It's green on the front, but black on the back, red on the right side, white on the left side.

---

[106] Gotham Books, 2007.

So, if you're standing over there you see his hat as being white, but I'm standing over here so I see his hat as being black, or as green or even red. And then pretty soon we get to arguing about which one of us is right and, sooner or later, the fists are flying!

Don't let Edshu play you like a sucker.

THE TRUTH ABOUT MAKING YOURSELF STRONGER

LXXIII.

Test yourself with fire and ice, sand and sea, **bile and blood, before your enemies do.**

Truths LXXIII through LXXVI are all about "strength". But this kind of strength has nothing to do with being able to bench-press more than Terry Crews.

Your enemies *are* going to "test" you. That's their job. Your job is to "test" yourself before they do:

"Fire is the test of gold; adversity, of strong men."

---Seneca, 4 BC- 65 AD

If you know you've got to take a test tomorrow, you study for it today, right? Always assume Life is going to test you about *something* tomorrow...and maybe *today!*

183

Know what you're capable of both physically and mentally...and then keep improving on that.

People like being "comfortable." But philosopher Friedrich Nietzsche warned that, no matter how "comfortable" you get, you have to keep "pushing against your walls", constantly testing yourself, constantly taking on fresh challenges.

Lifting the same weight day-after-day, we never grow any stronger.

*   *   *   *   *

In 9 AD, The Romans invaded into what's now Germany and got their asses handed to them by a strong young tribal leader named Arminius, aka "Herman the German".

Like Jugurtha and Spartacus before him, Arminius had at one time been trained by and had served with the Roman army.

He'd seen Rome's great strength and he'd seen the Romans' greater weaknesses first hand, so he knew the formula for defeating them:

> "If I have cunning of mind, I can gain strength of arm.
> If I have strength of arm, then I can lift a heavy stone. If
> I can lift a heavy stone, then I can take the sword from
> my enemy's hand. And if I can take the sword from my
> enemy's hand, I will have gained either an ally, or else
> gained a kingdom!"

> ---*The Arguments of Arminius*

LXXIV.

Pain is ever the best teacher.

Pain is only weakness leaving the body.

Death is only pain leaving the body.

Recall that Siddhartha Guatama, the Prince of India who gave away his great fortune to become a penniless monk and ultimately win the title of wise *Buddha* ("Enlightened One"), taught that we suffer pain because we want things we *don't need* and desire things we *can't get.*

He called this "The First Noble Truth".

So, if we can only stop chasing after things we *don't need* and *can't realistically get,* we'll be a much happier people, with a whole lot less pain in our lives.

So says The Buddha.

Of course, most of us are either too stubborn or else just not paying enough attention to Life--or both-and so we have to learn Life's lessons "the hard way".

And "the hard way" usually involves putting up with at least a little *pain.*

Someone can warn you not to stick your finger in a light-socket till they're blue in the face.

Stick your finger in that light-socket one time however and... you won't do *that* again!

Pain---and, all-too-often, *death-sure* have a way of getting peoples' attention. That's why Arminius once pointed out that "Men are made so much more by their pains than by their gains."

The good news is that, when a broken bone heals, it's always then twice as strong at the place it was broken.

⁎ ⁎ ⁎ ⁎ ⁎

"As old Patrick Henry said-! always like to quote Pat because when I was going to their school, they taught me to believe in it. They said he was a patriot. And he's the only one I quote. I don't know what any of the rest of them said. But I know what Pat said: Liberty or death. That means the ballot or the bullet. That's what it means in Harlemese, in Harlem talk...Brothers the price is death, really. The price to make others respect your human rights is death. You have to be ready to die or you have to be ready to take the lives of others. This is what old Patrick Henry meant when he said liberty of death. Life, liberty, and the pursuit of happiness, or kill me. Treat me like a man, or kill me. *11*

---Malcolm X, 1964[107]

LXXV.

A first taste of defeat, though bitter, goes far to prepare your palate for future feasts.

---

[107] Revolutionary War hero Patrick Henry (1736-1799) gave King George of England the finger by declaring "Give me liberty or give me death!"

In 1990, 42-1 underdog Buster Douglas, laid then -Heavyweight Champion of the World Mike Tyson out on the canvas in the 10th.

The world was stunned.

Up until then "Iron Mike", who in 1986 had become the youngest Heavyweight champion at barely 20 years old, had never been knocked out.

Shortly thereafter Mike Tyson went to prison for four years. That's all some people--haters at *least-want* to remember.

However, while in prison, Mike studied philosophy and psychology, mastered--and then taught-Anger & Stress Management to his fellow prisoners, and he embraced religion.

After being released[108] he briefly returned to·boxing just long enough to win back his WBC and WBA *belts.....by knockouts*

Having since retired from the ring, Mike Tyson now devotes his time to raising a family, helping others through his devotion to community service, and he has also gone on to gain respect as an actor, guest-starring on dozens of TV-shows and appearing in dozens of Hollywood hit movies.

Nine-times down. Ten times up.

*   *   *   *   *

---

[108] "Whatever Mike had done, he'd paid the price that a judge had determined was appropriate for his crime.
That's why we have law instead of mob rule." Evander Holyfield, Becoming *Holyfield: A Fighter's Journey* (Atria Books/NY 2008.

Henry Ford[109] Milton Hershey[110] Russell Simmons; Donald Trump and other financial wizards have all, at one time or another, seen their fortunes and futures disappear overnight. But such set-backs only made them tighten their belts, re-double their efforts, and come back even stronger-even *richer!* --the next time.

*   *   *   *   *

Despite the fact he was born into slavery[111] after the Civil War young Robert Church (1839-1912) started *a series of businesses*[112] including saloons, hotels, theaters, even banks.

All odds against him, despite many initial failures, many ups and downs, when most *Whites* in both the North and the South were still dirt-poor, Church succeeded in becoming the first African-American *millionaire* in the South.

His family would go on to become powerful leaders in the Southern branch of the Republican Party.

*   *   *   *   *

Down through history single individuals who refused to give up, from Spartacus to Nat Turner to Malcolm X and Nelson Mandela, have gone from actually breaking rocks in slave-pits and prisons to carving their names into the stone atop the mountain of history and making a positive difference in the lives of *millions* of others worldwide.

---

[109] Started the first Detroit Automobile Company in 1899. Went bankrupt in 1901, came back to become the most powerful businessman in the world.
[110] Founded the Hershey Chocolate Company in 1876, (the company that makes all those candy bars you eat!) went bankrupt in 1882 but, by 1900 was a millionaire.
[111] Anyone can be born *into* slavery...but no man is *born* a slave!
[112] That's what they mean by "Don't put all your eggs in one basket."

Likewise, across the centuries our ancestors have stoically sucked up the pain, crawling bravely through the mud and the blood under biting whips and hateful words, to ultimately ascend to great and honorable heights.

We shame their memory and belittle their accomplishments by daring to complain of our own *petty* day-to-day pains.

Nine times down. Ten times up!

> "Losing isn't the dirty word most fans-and a lot of athletes think it is. Losing is an important part of a competitive life. And while nobody enjoys losing, the trick isn't to be 100 percent perfect all the time. It's to deal with the occasional loss in ways that make it less painful and less counterproductive."
>
> -----Evander Holyfield (Ibid)

> "There are no failures, only quitters."
>
> -----Russell Simmons, 2007

LXXVI.

Discipline is ever an iron trap--be sure you are the one to set it in place.

Endeavor must exceed environment. You have to be stronger-and *smarter-than* the streets.

Growing up fast on the mean streets, Russell Simmons faced the same trials and tribulations and *temptations* every kid face:

"I began to get caught up with drugs and gangs-not because I was a bad person at heart, but because they seemed to be the most powerful ways for me to express myself in that environment."

---Russell Simmons, 2007

But Russell Simmons gained mastery over the streets...and then over *millions,* by first gaining mastery over himself, practicing such Eastern disciplines as yoga and meditation. (Ibid.)

Whatever it takes. By any means necessary. *Masakatsu!*

Think of this as a follow-up to Truth LXXIII.

*   *   *   *   *

"One of the best ways to get your mind in shape is through the practice of meditation. While physical exercise makes you stronger by building things up-- like muscle and stamina-the mental workout that you get through meditation makes you stronger by clearing things away. It clears away the distractions of the world and gives you the clarity to see and the focus to pursue the God-given visions that will be the foundation of your success. Building up your body or your bank account will bring you short-time happiness, but you can't take those things with you on your journey through life. No matter how many weights you lift, eventually your body will sag. No matter how much money you make, eventually it will lose its value and its appeal. But a clear and focused mind will last a lifetime. Getting your mind in shape is nothing less than the key to sustainable success in the world."

----Russell Simmons, 2007

THE TRUTH ABOUT FAMILY & FRIENDS

LXXVII.

The best hearth doubles as a **kiln.**

Given his great battlefield accomplishments, it's natural we think of Hannibal as an accomplished warrior and commander of men. But Hannibal was also a dedicated family man and loyal friend. That's why many of his 99 Truths, and not just this and the following four Truths, touch on the intimacy and influence those nearest and dearest exercise over us.

*   *   *   *   *

Ancient homes were always centered around a "hearth" (pronounced "harth"), an open fireplace, often circular and set in the middle of the main room, that not only lighted and heated the home, but which was also used as an oven for cooking.

Since the hearth was so important to the family, the word "hearth" soon came to mean "family".

A "kiln" is another kind of fireplace, a special oven where potters put their soft clay creations (cups, plates, etc.) to be hardened by the heat.

So what Hannibal is saying here is that our environment-our homelife in particular-should not only warm and feed us, but also *toughen* us up.

For example, after having revealed how dangerous it was for him growing up on the harsh, unforgiving streets of inner-city Chicago (see Truth VI), one of the best phrases in Isaiah Thomas' 2001 *The*

Fundamentals: 8 Plays for Winning the Games of Business and Life is where he describes his parents having "high expectations in spite of low circumstances" in their determination and dedication to helping their children succeed in life:

> "My parents, and especially my mother, understood that the deadliest killer in our neighborhood was not drugs, street gangs, or lack of nourishment, it was a poverty of dreams...My parents had high expectations in spite of low circumstances... We were taught to determine our own destinies, not to leave our lives up to other people, or circumstances, or simple luck. We were expected to swim, not go with the tide. The value system we learned was one in which we were held responsible for our own success. No one owed us a living, happiness, love, consideration, or appreciation. We had to earn those things. That is the way life works. If you expect money, good health, respect, or love to be handed to you, your expectations are way too high. Don't feel cheated if they aren't met. You've gotten what you deserved. If, however, you commit yourself to working hard, treating people the way you want to be treated and never giving up, you will probably be rewarded in ways you can't even dream." (Ibid.)

∗ ∗ ∗ ∗ ∗

"[My parents] have raised me well, and I truly believe they have taught me to accept full responsibility for all aspects of my life."

---Tiger Woods[113]

∗ ∗ ∗ ∗ ∗

---

[113] *18 Holes with Tiger* (Beckett Publications,1999)

"All kids need is a little help, a little hope, and somebody who believes in them.

-----Magic Johnson[114]

LXXVIII.

No one teaches my sons as well as my enemies.

Rome had a really bad-costly--habit of training its own enemies.

Rome trained Spartacus, *just* by forcing this Thracian warrior to serve in the Roman army then, after imprisoning him for deserting, training him to be even more dangerous as a slave-gladiator fighting to the death in the arena •

Spartacus "thanked" his Roman teachers by first slaughtering his own slave master and then leading a slave revolt that lasted three years and cost tens of thousands of Roman lives.

African king Jugurtha also trained with and fought beside the Romans, noting their every weakness[115] so that, when the time came, he easily defeated every Roman army sent against him. (See Truth LXXXI.)

Likewise, in 9 AD, Arminius, a tribal chief trained in the ways of war by the Romans and who had even risen to the exalted rank of Knight *(Equestrian)* in Roman society, successfully lured, trapped, and then massacred over 15,000 Roman soldiers in the thick forests of his native Germany.

---

[114] *My Life* by Earvin "Magic" Johnson with William Novak (Random House,1992)
[115] "Familiarity breeds contempt." --Aesop, The Ethiop.

Rome isn't the only one to make this mistake:

- Recall how the Egyptians trained and armed an elite army of Mameluk slaves who eventually rose up to overthrow their masters. (See Truth XXXV).

- Growing up as a royal hostage in the Islamic capital of Istanbul (now in Turkey) Christian Prince Vlad" Dracula" Tepes learned all the tactics of total war and terrible torture from his Muslim captors so well that, upon returning to his own kingdom as an adult, he quickly-deservedly!--earned the fearsome nickname "Vlad the Impaler" for turning those same terroristic cruelties against his former masters when they tried to invade his country again.

- And let's not forget Toussaint L'overture, the slave who rose to become a knowledgeable General in the French army...before using that same knowledge to free his nation from French overlords. (See Truth Ill.)

*   *   *   *   *

Sun Tzu warned that if you know yourself but don't know your enemy, you've cut your chances of winning in half.

Study your enemy, your opponent, your competition.

On the one hand, you might discover-hopefully in the nick of time! --that he's *twice* the danger you suspected him of being.

So, you can prepare.... *more.*

On the other hand, in studying your enemy, you might realize that he's not going to be *half the* problem you thought he was going to be.

So, you can relax...a little.

*   *   *   *   *

"People before have learned from their enemies."

> ---Aristophanes, Greek Philosopher
> 450-385 BC

*   *   *   *   *

"We can learn even from our enemies."

> ---Ovid 43 BC- 18 AD

"The haft of the arrow had been feathered with one of the eagle's · own plumes. How often we give our enemies the means of our own destruction."

> ---Aesop, The Ethiop

LXXIX.

All that is required of a father is to teach his sons patience. Sons, by their very nature, teach their fathers patience.

Hannibal, Spartacus, Jugurtha, Shaka Zulu, Toussaint L'overture, and a hundred other successful leaders all had to have one thing before they could accomplish everything else: *patience*.

Patience takes (I) determination and (2) discipline.

History records how, with enough determination and discipline, men have won great fame and wealth, built mighty empires, cured disease, mapped the four comers of the Earth, and walked on the moon.

Where the wiseman is *patient,* the fool *is* a patient.

*　*　*　*　*

"The greatest gift a father can pass along to his son isn't a magic sword with which to slay all his enemies, nor a vast kingdom, not even great wealth. The greatest gift a father *must* pass along to his son is *patience.* For only patience makes all these others possible!"

--Arminius

*　*　*　*　*

"I like the idea of being a role model. It's an honor. People took the time to help me as a kid, and they impacted my life. I want to do the same for kids."

----Tiger Woods

LXXX.

Mirrors tell the cruelest tales.

A good mirror never shows the same reflection twice. Can you remember your face before we had mirrors? The face of a friend is the truest mirror.

This Truth speaks to our ability to (I) see ourselves truthfully (as if looking in the mirror), and (2) our being *blessed* enough to have family and friends-a *posse-who* helps keep us grounded.

There's a big difference between people who care enough about you to help keep you "grounded" (looking at the world realistically) and others who just try to put you down.

Prince Vlad Tepes saw it this way:

> "When I look in the mirror, I see no reflection!
>
> Where I walk, no shadow hounds me! Were other men so fortunate."[116]

Prince Vlad was saying that no man is his equal when it comes to courage and cunning...at least not his enemies.

According to Nietzsche, all men come out of the womb equal...but, after that, they part company!

It's all about making the most of what you've been *given-unique* insights that exist in each of us in different concentration and combinations.

Each of us has within us-from birth-all the courage we'll ever need to deal with any threat life tries throwing at us.

In addition, we're all fully capable of developing all the cunning we'll ever need to deal with any competition we might run into in any ring we decide to climb into.

We only need learn to tell the difference between a "threat" and "competition".

Even the stupidest man on *Earth--especially* the stupidest man on Earth! ---can be a "threat" to you, his stupidity and ignorance just an accident waiting to happen, waiting to drag you down with him

---

[116] *Lost Arts of War (Citadel Press, 2012)*

Avoid such people:

"Competition", on the other hand, is anyone trying to give you a run for your money, anyone whose ability or product has the potential to interfere with, outshine, or otherwise out-sell *your* ability and/or product.

Study such people.

The goal is to (I) *eliminate* all "threats", and (2) *limit "competition"*.

A "little" competition is useful for keeping us current and on our toes. Truth VI again.

Never pass up an opportunity to learn from your competition.

On the other hand, *never* tolerate a "threat".

* * * * *

At the entrance to the *Ka'aba* temple in the holy city of Mecca hang 7 poems, one of them written by a black African warrior named Antar, his Arabic name being "Abu!Fouaris"[117]

Antar was born into slavery in the year 525 AD yet he died a King 90 years later, killed in battle by poisoned arrows.

In between, Antar's many adventures, as recorded in *The Romance of Antar,* became the inspiration for many of the heroes in the classic *1001 Arabian Knights,* a 19th century collection of stories in English taken from much older African and Arabian sources and re-written by European explorer Sir Richard Francis Burton (1821-1890)[118]

---

[117] *Dirty Little Secrets about Black History, It's Heroes, and Other Troublemakers by* Claude Anderson, Ed.D. @ www.powernomics.com. 1997
[118] Burton is reportedly the only non-Muslim to ever visit-in disguise-the holy city of Mecca and live!

You've already heard about, read about, and seen all kinds of movies made about many of these Antar-inspired heroes, including Aladdin (and his magic lamp); Ali Baba (whose cunning outwitted The Forty Thieves); and Sindbad the Sailor, whose 7 voyages took him around the world long before Columbus.

Antar's adventures began while he was just a young boy, still a slave, when he won his freedom by saving the life of his Arab King slave master from an assassin.

But Antar didn't use a sword or spear to save the King, he used a *mirror*. While working as a servant boy in the palace, Antar overheard one of the King's advisors plotting with an assassin to kill the King. Antar then secretly watched as the treacherous Advisor hid his assassin in a secret room behind the King's throne where all knew the King would be sitting during the feast planned for that night.

Though young, Antar knew that if the King was killed conditions for him and the other slaves would be much worse under the rule of the much crueler Advisor.

But, also knowing that the word of a "mere slave" would never be believed over the word of the King's "trusted" Advisor, the young boy wondered what to do.

Finally, Antar came up with a plan. And he began polishing the big silver platter he always used when serving the King food.

That night, while the feast was in full swing, Antar watched until he saw the hidden door behind the King start to inch open. Immediately Antar walked up to the throne and held the shiny *empty* silver platter out to the confused King.

"Why is there *nothing* on your platter, slave? The King asked.

"Nothing...except the rest of your life, Sire," Antar replied, holding the shining silver platter higher until the King could see his own confused face reflected there...and *the assassin right behind him raising a dagger!*

The King jumped out of the way just in the nick of time.

The assassin was quickly captured by the King's guards and just as quickly snitched out the evil Advisor's role in the plot.

For his part in saving the King, Antar was rewarded with not only his freedom but also the freedom of his fellow Abs tribesmen.

Welcomed home and hailed as a hero by his Abs tribesmen, since his own parents were dead, Antar was adopted by the Abs chieftain.

As the years passed *Prince* Antar would prove his courage and cunning again and again in a hundred battles and adventures, eventually becoming King himself.

And every day, from the first day he became king until his dying day, King Antar took time to look into that same shining platter (given him as a parting gift by the grateful Arab King he had saved), kept hanging in his throne room and used as a mirror...and as a reminder to always be a good King.

LXXXI.

The enemy of my enemy is my friend.

———————————

In *the Prince* (1513), Machiavelli answers the question of whether it's better for a ruler to be *feared or loved* Machiavelli said it's better for a prince to be feared because fear is always the same and remains constant--once you kick someone's ass it *stays* kicked!

Love on the other hand, says Machiavelli, can turn to hate at any time, in an instant, for the least little reason.

In other words, today's buddy might be tomorrow's back-stabber!

The good news in this also works the opposite way: If you play your cards right, today's enemy just might be tomorrow's *friend*. Remember Truth XLV?

During his long career, Hannibal had many allies, most who remained loyal to him, even fighting to the death for him. These allies even included some European tribes like the Gauls (from what is now France and Spain) who hated Rome as much as Harmibal's people did.

Most of Hannibal's allies however were his fellow Africans, like the much-feared Libyan spearmen and the fierce bare-back riding horsemen who came from the large North African kingdom of Numidia just to the south of Carthage.

Numidia was a prosperous African nation, feared and respected by its neighbors. During the 1st and and Punic Wars between Rome and Carthage Numidia supplied grain and other food and textiles to Carthage.

In addition, Numidian cavalry, horsemen and war-elephants, made up a large part of Carthage's army,

When Hannibal invaded into Italy, he left half his army in Spain under the command of his brothers Hasdrubal and Mago.

This included over 4000 cavalrymen, the best of which were Numidian light horse fighters and war-elephants led by Masinissa, the King of Numidian.

The Numidians fighting with Hannibal, first in Spain and then in Italy, had always been loyal, helping Hannibal win many battles, and even saving his life a time or two.

However, in 204 BC Hannibal's Roman nemesis Scipio invaded North Africa as part of a plan to get Hannibal's army to leave Italy and quickly return to Africa to save Carthage.

Before invading Africa however, Scipio convinced Carthage's long-time ally King Masinissa of Numidia to come over to the Roman side.

Many felt King Masinissa only did what he had to in order to save his own people from being wiped out by the invading Europeans who would surely come for Numidia once they were finished with Hannibal's people.

Others saw Masinissa as a scheming opportunist in the right place at the right time to enlarge his kingdom by betraying a former ally.

Masinissa believed Carthage was going to lose. Afterall, Rome had already beaten Carthage once in the I" Punic War.

By defecting to Rome, Numidia would not only save it's own lands but also be able to claim a large chunk of Carthage land after the war.

Many Nurnidians didn't condone such treachery but feared rising against Masinissa so long as he had the backing of the powerful Romans.

News traveled so slow in those days that Nurnidian troops in Italy were still fighting and dying for Hannibal long after King Masinissa had went over to the Romans.

After the 2nd Punic War, the Romans used Masinissa to help keep Carthage in check, to keep Carthage from growing too powerful again.

After Carthage was destroyed at the end of the 3rd Punic War, Numidians began supplying their new ally Rome with men and material. For example, when Rome invaded Greece during The Macedonian War (172-168 BC), the Romans won with the help of Numidian war-elephants.

Masinissa died early during the 3rd Punic War and his son Micipsa became King of Numidia.

King Micipsa continued to provide grain, horsemen, and war-elephants to Rome. More importantly, he sent his trusted young nephew (and adopted son) *Jugurtha* in command of African war-elephants to Spain to help Roman Commander Aemilianus (185-129 BC) against the Numantia people who were rebelling against Rome.

It was during this Spanish campaign that Jugurtha, already a respected warrior, mastered the art of war, winning high praise for his courage and skill from friend and *future* foe alike:

> "...the Romans were fond of declaring that their most dangerous opponents were always those who they had trained themselves, just as Jugurtha had learned how to fight when serving with Aemilianus at Numantia.
>
> -Adrian Goldsworth, 2004[119]

In 118 BC Jugurtha was called home to Africa when his adopted father King Micipsa unexpectedly died.

Jugurtha suddenly found himself at the center of a controversy when it was revealed that Miscipsa's will decreed that the Kingdom of Numidia should be ruled *jointly* by his adopted son Jugurtha (whom he knew to be a great military commander) and his two natural sons (whom he knew to be scheming politicians).

Miscipsa had been smart enough to know that, when dealing with a powerful *potential enemy* like Rome, it's always wise to have a scheme or two (Adherbal and Hiempsal) in on one hand while always keeping a sharp sword (Jugurtha) in your other hand!

Unfortunately for Numidia, this royal arrangement was doomed to failure from the beginning..

---

[119] *In the Name of Rome: The Men Who Won the Roman Empire* (Phoenix Paperback, US: 2004:69)

After Hiempsal (probably with Adherbal's blessing) sent assassins to murder Jugurtha, Jugurtha took pleasure in *personally* killing Hiempsal.

Adherbal immediately fled to Rome for help.

As Machiavelli has pointed out, anytime you have two (or more princes) and only *one* empty throne, there's bound to be bloodshed. History shows this happening time and again in Europe, in Japan, even in China.

African princes are no exception.

Look at the warring between Cleopatra and her brother over the throne of Egypt. And keep in mind that even the great Shaka Zulu was killed by rival princes, his own step-brothers.

Similar struggles between princes and other members of the royal family were common amongst the Numidian and Moorish royal houses in North Africa. In fact, one of the ways King Masinissa justified (at least in his own mind) betraying Hannibal was because he needed Rome to back his claim to being the one legitimate ruler of Numidia. (Ibid.)

Worried that a civil war in Africa between Princes Jugurtha and Abherbal would interfere with grain and other wealth coming into Rome from ports in North Africa, the Roman Senate declared that the kingdom of Numidia should be *divided* equally between the two Numidian princes.

Rather than see his nation broken apart by Rome, Jugurtha and his army immediately attacked and captured Adherbal's new capital city Cirta. Unfortunately, during the siege of Cirta, Jugurtha's warriors slaughtered a group of Roman businessmen operating there.

This killing of Roman citizens so outraged The Senate that they declared Jugurtha an outlaw and immediately sent a general named Bestia to invade North Africa and restore peace by bringing Jugurtha to *justice-Roman justice.*

Still trying to avoid all-out war with Rome, Jugurtha played diplomat and arranged to travel to Rome under a flag of true.

Familiar with Roman politics, Jugurtha immediately got busy using Numidia's vast wealth to blatantly bribe a bunch of *influential-greedy!* -Senators into voting in his favor.

Fortune seemed to be finally smiling in Jugurtha's direction until it was discovered he'd taken time out from his busy schedule bribing Senators to kill another member of the Numidian royal family who had fled to Rome for protection after siding with Adherbal.

Now Romans were used to political rivals assassinating one another. In fact, Romans kind of *expected* that sort of thing. After all, in 44 BC, a group of Senators would band together to stab Julius Caesar to death *in* the Senate itself!

But when word got out how Jugurtha had "attempted" to bribe "honest" Senators, Roman citizens were suddenly calling for the African princes' head!

As he escaped Rome, in disgust Jugurtha declared:

> "Rome is a city up for sale and it will surely perish if it
> ever finds a buyer!"

Easily eluding Romans soldiers sent to capture him, Jugurtha returned to Africa with a price on his head, now openly rebelling against Rome.

When the Roman Commander Bestia proved unable to catch up with let alone capture Jugurtha, he was replaced by a Roman Commander named Albinus.

A wilier opponent that Bestia, Albinus immediately hit Jugurtha where it hurt: *in his wallet.*

Albinus lay siege (encircled) Jugurtha's fortress city of Suthul, where the African prince kept his main treasury.

Outnumbered and stalling for time, Jugurtha pretended to negotiate with Albinus until he could thin out Albinus' army by secretly bribing the Ligurian[120] and Thracian[121] mercenaries in Albinus' army into deserting.

Jugurtha then bribed a Roman *Centurian* (officer) in Albinus' army into leaving the gate to Albinus' camp open, allowing Jugurtha to stage a surprise night attack on Albinus' camp that panicked the Roman army.

Those Romans who didn't run away, including Albinus, were captured. But, instead of killing Albinus and his soldiers, Jugurtha spared their lives in return for Albinus (who was authorized to speak for the Senate) declaring him to be the rightful *sole* ruler of Numidia.

Albinus agreed and Jugurtha let him and his Legionaires go-but only after the Romans gave up all their weapons and were then forced to march out of Numidia under an arch created by raised African spears-an ancient African shaming ritual that shows that a man has lost his honor and his "warrior" status. Angered by this humiliation of their soldiers, the Roman Senate tore up the peace treaty forced on Albinus and, instead, gave the disgraced Albinus' command in Africa to a cruel and cunning veteran Roman commander named Metellus.

Quickly realizing he was up against a more ruthless opponent, Jugurtha used the old Hannibal ploy of refusing to fight the full Roman army out in the open (where they were strongest). Instead, Jugurtha fought the Romans guerrilla-style: appearing where least expected; attacking in smaller, fast-moving groups; and then disappearing back into the countryside before the Romans even knew what hit them!

---

[120] **Now southern France.**
[121] Now in modern Bulgaria, where the gladiator/rebel slave leader Spartacus came from.

But, having studied Hannibal's tactics himself, Metellus knew how to force Jugurtha out into battle.

Knowing that like all guerrilla fighters Jugurtha depended on the support of his people, Metellus began a savage "scorched earth" policy of burning down to the ground any city or village loyal to Jugurtha.

Metellus' plan worked.

Enraged and wanting to save his people from further harm, Jugurtha attacked Metellus' Roman army with a large force including war-elephants as the Romans marched across open country near the River Muthul.

Though Jugurtha's fierce attack inflicted heavy casualties on the Romans, the Africans were finally forced to withdraw after too many of their war-elephants were killed.

Within days, Metellus' went back to attacking Jugurtha loyalist towns and burning their vital crops.

True to Roman tradition, Metellus' hedged his bets by trying to bribe Jugurtha's people into betraying him no luck.

Metellus also tried hiring hit-men to take a contract on the African prince. Suicide mission. Again, *no takers.*

Like Bestia before him, all Metellus' efforts failed.

Dissatisfaction was growing in Rome with how slow "The Jugurtha Campaign" was going and with how North African grain and other fabulous wealth normally flowing into Rome from Africa was being disrupted.

It didn't help then when Marius, an ambitious officer serving under Metellus, accused his superior of deliberately prolonging the war in order to further his own political ambitions.

This all came to a head for Metellus when all the African-born soldiers serving in a Roman garrison at the Numidian town of Vaga defected, first killing their Roman officers, then joining the citizens declaring the town for Jugurtha.

To his credit, Metellus quickly recaptured the city, not with overwhelming force but by taking a page from Hannibal's playbook.

Putting Numidian cavalry still allied with Rome at the head of his army, Metellus tricked the citizens of Vaga into opening wide their gates, letting the Romans in before the citizens of Vaga realized their-fatal! mistake.

Despite this Roman "victory", the ambitions Marius was still able to use this Vaga disaster to convince the Senate to allow him to replace Metellus as commander in Africa.

Immediately Marius ran into the same problems the three Roman commanders before him had.

It took Marins another 3-years to finally end the war.

Methodical, one-by-one Marins destroyed all the towns and fortresses supporting Jugurtha, tightening the noose until finally trapping the African prince in his last stronghold near the river Mulaccha.

After the fierce fighting, the fortress at Mulaccha finally fell. But it was a hollow victory for Marins when he discovered that Jugurtha had slipped the noose yet again!

Determined to regroup and return to liberate Numidia from the Romans, Jugurtha escaped west to the lands of Numidia's *supposed* ally, King Bocchus of Mauretania.

But, unbeknownst to Jugurtha, Bocchus had already sold him out... and the Romans were waiting.

Jugurtha went down fighting.

And, in the end, he took a lot of Rome's reputation for "invincibility" down with him:

> "The war with the Numidian King Jugurtha (112-106 BC) resulted in scandals as [Roman] troops deserted in masse, and [Roman] commanders were found to be either incompetent or had been bribed by the enemy. The first Roman army sent to the war surrendered and suffered the humiliation of being sent under the yoke."

> ---Adrian Goldsworthy
> *Roman warfare, 2005*[122]

LXXXII.

Men are never as helpless, nor as clever as they believe themselves to be.

In his 2007 *Do You!* Russell Simmons tells us that one of his favorite quotes is "A man's strength is to know his weakness,"

This is pure Sun Tzu. Pure Hannibal. *Pure...any* true leader! Back to" The Three Knows":

- *Know yourself;*

- *Know your enemy* (opponent, competition);

---

[122] Smithsonian Books

- *Know your environment* (your surroundings, your street...your cellblock). If you're incapable of taking a realistic assessment of yourself-your wants and desires, assets and liabilities-then what chance do you have of ever getting inside your opponent's head?

If you're so blind you can't scope out your own self-defeating actions and notice how *ignore-ant* you're acting when you continue to slam the doors of opportunity because of your juvenile "need" for needless noise and attention,[123] then what chance are you going to have of ever noticing what's going on around you, let alone being able to figure out what's going on inside your enemy's head?

* * * * *

"Perhaps you're tougher than you've let on and owe yourself some overdue credit.

---Chris Gardner
The Pursuit of Happyness, 2006

THE TRUTH ABOUT WIT & WISDOM

LXXXIII.

Wit is the sharpest of swords but the thinnest of shields.

There's nothing wrong with being *erudite* (our fancy word for the day).

---

[123] **"You're only young once. But you can be immature forever."** *Mahogany, 1975*

So much of good communication is simply picking the right word, the right turn of phrase, with just the right *inflection* (a fancy word we'll save for tomorrow).

Everybody likes a smart person, someone who expresses himself or herself well, who speaks directly and forcefully when necessary, someone whose ideas help get the job done--ideas that help all of us get rich and stay that way!

On the other hand, nobody likes a smart ass.

Nobody likes a liar who just makes facts up as he goes along. So:

- *Get the facts.* Use the sources of information available to you...and always be on the lookout for additional sources of information. Always cross-check your facts to see if your sources "agree".

- *Keep your facts straight.* Don't make shit up, "filling in the blanks" to make your information seem more important than it really is.

- *Practice presenting your facts* in a clear and concise manner, whether in written or video form, and especially in public speaking form.

Back in the old days people had no choice but to rely on their memories or, later on, scribbles on post-it notes. As a result, disagreements were predictable, arguments inevitable, and violence all, too, too when people "remembered" the same thing from different angles. That "3 Blind men and the elephant" syndrome again.

Nowadays there's no excuses (and hopefully no need for violence) since we now literally have the answer to what team won what Superbowl which year and how many points out favorite NBA player scored last season, at our fingertips--on our iPhone, or on our laptop.

Being "smart" isn't about *knowing everything,* it's about knowing *where to find everything.* And that includes whatever facts and information you need at any given minute to help you get to where you want to be the next minute, next year, and the next level of your life.

There's an app for that.

There's also an ancient Chinese saying:

"When the student is ready is ready the teacher will appear."

Sometimes that "teacher" is an actual person. Other times your "teacher" might be the inspiring or inciting lyrics from a song, or simply a passage you read in a book.

The good news is we no longer have to go to the library, someone's brought the library to us:

> "Our people are still walking the streets frustrated, when there's a library on the corner they could be walking into instead and using what they find there to improve themselves. Trust me, the doors to those libraries have not always been open. Just like the doors to the radio stations and TV networks and record labels and gated communities and universities have not always been open either. Even though pioneers had to pry those doors open for us, we still won't walk through them. That's very frustrating to the previous generations who fought such a terrible fight for use."

> ----Russell Simmons, 2007

LXXXIV.

The words we weave today bind us to tomorrow

In case you missed the e-mail: You're 100% responsible for every word that comes out your pie-hole.

If you *said* it yesterday...that better be what you're *doing* today.

*   *   *   *   *

"People have the power we give them. Words have the power we give them."

---Whoopi Goldberg, 1997

LXXXV.

Today's lie, tomorrow's test of memory.

When "Honest Abe" Lincoln warns us, we might want to pay attention:

"No man has a good enough memory so as to be a convincing liar."

LXXXVI.

Truth makes a fine philter but a meager meal.

A "philter" is a medicine. Something that cures you. The saying goes that "The truth will set you free."

True that. But that doesn't mean the truth is always going to make you *happy.*

Do you really want to know that the love of your life is screwing around on you? Do you really want to find out you're HIV+?

There's a lot of "truth" people *don't* want to know. The Bible says Jesus was filled with "truth *and* grace."

"Grace", in this case, means knowing *when* and *how* to tell the truth, like giving people bad news.

- We want people to agree with us.

- We like people to agree with us.

- We like people who agree with us.

- Big surprise! People sometimes *act* like they agree with us just to get close to us, just to get what they want.

As a result, telling people the truth, the whole truth, and nothing but the truth isn't always high on everyone's "to do" list.

It should be high on *your* list however.

* * * * *

"Never forget that truth rings a bell that the whole world can hear. A truth that will bring you more fans, more customers, and more love than you ever imagined possible."

---Russell Simmons, 2007

LXXXVII.

Tradition makes a fine footstool but a poor ladder.

There's nothing wrong with honoring the tried-n-true traditions of our ancestors.

Celebrating the ways and wisdom of our forefathers who founded those traditions helps us connect with our roots, helping us better understand-and—*claim*! --our rightful place on history. That is, *unless* a "tradition"--ours, or someone else's-holds us back, keeping us from embracing *new and better* traditions:

> "We feel the spirit of our ancestors who challenge us to
> be more than what white society gives us as standards
> and limitations."

> ----Sister Souljah[124]

After all, *slavery* was a "tradition" the United States of America from 1776 untill862.

It's not surprising then that many of the great men and women movers and shakers down though history have made a "tradition" of *breaking* tradition.

Shaka Zulu for example.

*   *   *   *   *

---

[124] Ibid. 1996

Shaka Zulu (1787-1828) has been called "The greatest military genius Africa has yet known.[125]

Zulu chiefs practiced polygamy. This helped ensure that the chief would have strong sons to carry on his linage and also provided stability to the tribe, since the people knew that when a strong chief died or was killed in battle an equally strong chief would take his place.

Unfortunately, having sons by more than one wife often led to underhanded scheming on the part of ambitious mothers wanting *their* son to become chief, and led to sometimes violent disputes among competing princes.

As a result, though born the son of a (Zulu clan chief, Shaka's early life reminds us a lot of the story of Ishmael and his Egyptian mother Hagar in the Bible[126]

When haters and schemers falsely accused Shaka's mother (to whom Shaka was totally devoted) of having conceived him through incest, the two of them were despised and ultimately driven from their home.

As a result, again like Ishmael, "Burning with revenge"[127], Shaka became a soldier in the army on King Dingiswayo of the Mthethwa people (who at the time ruled over the smaller Zulu clan).

Thanks to his courage and cunning, Shaka rose quickly through the ranks until, by the age of 22, Shaka had already become one of King Dingiswayo's trusted war-chiefs.

Faced with a threat from the ruthless Zwideto, chief of the nearby Ndwandwethe tribe, Dingiswayo and the Mthethwa were forced to go to war, but were unltimately defeated at the Battle of Mbuzu Hill, where Dingiswayo was killed and his army routed.

---

[125] *Millennium Year by Year* Commemorative Edition, 2000:469.
[126] Genesis Chapters 6-21.
[127] *Millennium Year by Year,* 2000.

Wounded, Shaka survived the battle, avoided enemy hunters and eventually made his way back to his own people.

Word of Shaka's warrior heroics while serving King Dingiswayo had already reached his people, and his status among Zulu grew.

By the time his father died in I 818, Shaka's supporting faction had grown powerful enough to defeat the faction favoring his elder half-brother Singukana and declare Shaka chief.

Shaka wasted no time putting his new-found power to work.

Within the year, Zulus under Shaka's command had reconquered King Dingiswayo's old kingdom and defeated the Ndwandwe at the Battle of Mhlatuuze River in the Natal region (now South Africa).

Under Shaka's leadership, the Zulu Empire was soon dominating the entire Natal area, either absorbing or else driving out all other tribes: the *Hlubi; Khumalo; Ngwaneni; Mokoteli;* and the *Xhosa-speaking Tembu,* the tribe Nelson Mandela would be born into.[128]

A final Zulu victory over the last of the Ndwandwe in 1828 left Shaka in command of the largest empire ever seen in southern Africa.

Shaka declared a "No-man's land" between his growing empire in the north Natal and the increasing number of Europeans in the south.[129]

According to one biographer, Shaka's genius, the secret to his success, lay in his "attention to detail", *(Millennium Year by Year,* 2000) and in his willingness to innovate.

When it came to winning, Shaka had that "tradition of breaking tradition". For example, upon becoming chief, he made it Zulu law that

---

[128] The Zulu speak a language derived from the *Bantu* language. *Swahili* (language of East Africa) and the *Kikuyu* language (of Kenya) also come from Bantu.
[129] At about this same time The American Colonialization Society was setting up a homeland for freed U.S. Slaves in west Africa, founding the nation of Liberia.

a young Zulu couldn't get married and become a father until he had proven himself as a man and as a warrior[130]

Shaka also encouraged Zulu healers to travel far and wide collecting natural herbal cures and plant medicines that not only helped the Zulu people as a whole, but especially helped increase a warrior's confidence and strength, as well as dull the pain for wounded warriors and speed their healing.[131]

Also recall (from Truth XLV) how Shaka made provisions to take care of the family of any of his warriors killed in battle.

Knowing their families would be taken care of if they should fall in battle made Shaka's warriors even more loyal to him. See Truth XXII.

To further strengthen the Zulu army. Shaka banned the clumsy sandles Zulu men usually wore. Instead, he ordered Zulu warriors to train barefoot. As a result, Shaka soon had his warriors able to run over 50 miles a day, allowing his army to appear where least expected, faster than any other army.

He then organized the Zulu army into rival *impis,* regiments that competed to outdo one another, to run faster and longer, and to be first into battle.

You could tell which impis a warrior belonged to by each impis' distinctive feathered headdress, and by the different markings on the hide-shield all Zulu warriors carried (used defensively for protection and used offensively to strike an opponent off-balance and to block his line of sight).

Each Zulu warrior was required to master using the short-handled Zulu stabbing spear called an *assegai* (sometimes spelled "assegais").

---

[130] *Shaka Zulu,* E.A. Ritter,1955.
[131] See *Warriors* (Rubicon Publishing, Inc. 2006)

Each Zulu warrior carried several long assegai for throwing, along with a shorter assegai he used like a sword when close to an enemy.

> "A gun is a coward's weapon and a man have to be able to fight with assegais. If a man is a man, he will fight at close quarters."
>
> ---Zulu warrior Mangwanana Mcunu[132]

Some Zulu also carried a deadly hard wooden club known as a *knobkerrie*.

Most important, so far as the army was concerned, Shaka drilled his lieutenant's in the use of a strategy called "The Cow's Horns" (a variation of Hannibal's classic "envelopment" strategy) where the center of an attacking Zulu force (the cow's "head") slammed into an enemy force directly, while the cow's "horns" circled around and in from both sides to surround (envelop) the enemy.

Hannibal had used this same maneuver to defeat the Roman army at the Battle of Cannae.

Using this strategy, no one dared challenge the Zulu army in the field.

A popular ruler amongst his people, no one dared *openly* challenge Shaka to his face.

Behind his back was another matter.

On September 22, 1828, Shaka was assassinated by his half-brothers Dingane and Mhlangane.

*   *   *   *   *

---

[132] *World History of Warfare* by Christian I. Archer, et, AL, University of Nebraska Press, 2002:462.

Other kings led the Zulu nation after Shaka, but all kept his new "traditions". By the time of the last great Zulu War of 1879, the Zulu army was the most feared fighting force in Africa:

> "The Zulu nation certainly possessed the most efficient and potentially dangerous native army in Africa. It's soldiers, fit, athletic and trained for war from boyhood, were not allowed to marry until they proved themselves. As a result of this the younger units possessed a keen psychological edge induced by frustration and were naturally inclined to welcome war as a means of ending their enforced celibacy. The regiments were well organized, strictly disciplined and developed high *espirit de corps* which they demonstrated with individual titles, distinctive head plumes, shield markings and other adornments. On the march, regiments moved at a ground-devouring lope which often disrupted their opponent's plans before they were fully laid, and over broken country they could move faster than a horse. Their commanders were adept at concealing large bodies of men until the moment chosen for the attack had arrived." (Last *Stand! Famous Battles against the Odds* by Bryan Perrett. Cassell Military Paperbacks. London 1991:65)

By the 1879 war, some Zulu warrior carried firearms (mostly rifles), but the majority still preferred fighting "Zulu-style": getting close in and stabbing an enemy with an assegai. In a tactical variation of Shaka's "Cow's Head" strategy, Zulu warriors often worked in pairs, with one Zulu engaging a soldier in front while a second warrior circled around to stab or club him from behind.

* * * * *

The last Zulu war started in 1877 when the British Empire took over the lands in southern Africa bordering Zululand which had previously been occupied by Dutch Europeans called *Boers*.

Intimidated by the fact that Zulu King Cetewayo had an army of 40,000 warriors, the British demanded that Cetewayo disband the Zulu army.

Cetewayo refused.

The Zulu army was central to the Zulu way of life. Besides, laying down their weapons would leave the Zulu people at the mercy of the British who still had weapons, similar to the way American Native Americans were first disarmed and then placed on reservations, or the way swords were taken from the Samurai warriors of Japan.[133]

Or, as Malcolm X said:

> "If you have a dog, I must have a dog. If you have a rifle,
> I must have a rifle. If you have a club, I must have a club.
> That's equality."[134]

When Cetewayo refused, 15,000 British troops (6,000 Europeans and 9,000 native troops) violated Shaka's "No-man's land" and invaded into Zululand.

The patient Zulu army commander Matyana allowed the British to advance deep into Zulu territory and to even begin setting up camp that night at a place called Isandhlwana without attacking them.

"Put your spies far out! The Zulus are more dangerous than you think!" warned veteran Zulu fighter and guide J.J. Uys, but the British Commander wouldn't listen to him.

The British were armed with modem rifles and with 20 canons and I 0 rocket launchers,[135] while the Zulu were only armed with "primitive" weapons, so the British commander was overconfident.

---

[133] See the 2003 movie *The Last Samurai*.
[134] Ibid. Pathfinder, 1978.
[135] Perrett, 1991:67

He didn't know that during the night Matyana and his two lieutenants, a veteran Zulu commander named Tshingwayo and a younger leader named Mavumengwana, had hidden an army of 20,000 warriors in a nearby valley ready to strike.

At dawn what's been described as "a black wave more than a mile long...deployed twelve deep on a front of several miles" attacked the British.[136]

"The king didn't send us here to run away!

Mavumengwana yelled to his warriors as he led the charge against the British.

"Gi-di! Gi-di!", his warriors chanted in return, "Kill! Kill!"

Though the Zulu themselves would later compliment the British on how well the Redcoats fought, by mid-afternoon the battle was over and 1329 British troops lay dead.

Estimates of Zulu dead were between 2000 to 3000.

Though the British would later accuse Zulus of mutilating British bodies by slashing open bellies of the dead, Zulus actually did this in the belief that this helped release the souls of the dead.[137]

A few British troops survived by playing dead.

Soon after the Battle of Isandhlwana,[138] a little further down the road, 4,500 Zulus also attacked a British outpost at a place called Roake's Drift of 139 men.[139]

---

[136] Ibid. 76-77.
[137] The Japanese also believe the soul resides in the lower belly *{hara}*, this is why a Samurai cuts open his abdomen when committing *hara-kiri,* honorable suicide.
[138] See the 1979 movie *Zulu Dawn.*
[139] See the 1964 movie *Zulu.*

The British defenders were able to hold out against wave after wave of Zulu attack, including being fired on by Zulu sharpshooters before the Zulu broke off their attack.

Military experts maintain that, had the Zulu chosen, they could have continued the attack, eventually killing all the British at Roake's Drift but that (1) the brave defenders had earned the Zulus respect for their courage--warrior to warrior-and, (2) the Zulu left them alive so they could warn other Europeans what the cost was for daring to step foot in Zululand.

LXXXVIII.

A single thrust to the heart saves a thousand cuts to the limbs.

This Truth reminds us of Truth XXXIX, where Hannibal spoke from experience that "War should be swift, peace swifter still." and Truth XLIV:" If it began with a word, it can be ended with a word. If it began with the sword, the sword will surely end with it."

The ancient Romans had their own version of deadly "drone strikes", targeting an enemy rebel leader of king personally rather than allow a costly wide-scale war to continue.

Recall how African King Jugurtha was ultimately betrayed by a bribe.

At one time Rome reportedly turned down' an offer to have their German nemesis Arminius poisoned,[140] and later Rome would become

---

[140] *The Battle that Stopped Rome* by Peter S. Wells. (W.W. Norton & Company, NY-London, 2003)

the number one suspect for bankrolling the assassination (by poison) of their enemy Attila the Hun[141]

The modem English word "Assassin" comes from "Hashishin", a *ninja-like* 12th century Middle Eastern Muslim cult,[142] whose Grandmaster Hasan ibn Sabbah (aka "The Old Man of the Mountain") believed all the world's problems could be settled either through *education* or *assassination*.

Anyone standing in the way of Hasan's plans would wake up one morning to find an Assassin's dagger stuck into the pillow next to their head. Usually this "education" part of the program worked. When it didn't, there was always "assassination" to fall back on.[143]

This same successful "education or assassination" formula has continued to work down through history, since ancient times,[144] down to modern times.

Josef Stalin remained the undisputed-much feared-dictator of Russia for 50 years by following this same sinister philosophy. Any time Stalin was told someone was opposing his plans, he told his KGB agents "No man, no problem!"....and that man was never seen again!

This philosophy also worked for Idi Amin Dada, "President for Life" of Uganda, and for many other powerful---and *ruthless---20*[th] century politicians and power-brokers.

Sun Tzu I 01: Take care of those little problems (including problem people) before they have a chance to become big problems.

---

141 *The Night Attila Died by* Michael A. Babcock, 2005.

142 Remember: *Cult* is what the big church calls the little church.

143 For the complete history, tactics, and techniques of the cult of the assassins, see *Assassin/ Secrets of the Cult of the Assassins* by Dr, Haha Lung (Citadel Press, 2006).

144 "I have within me two gods, *persuasion* and *compulsion*." (Themistocles, Greek philosopher 528·462 BC)

Consider: A single bullet from Seal Team Six saved the word a lot of problems in the future.

Taking it down a notch: If you have a disgruntled employee today, find out what's bothering him before he becomes tomorrow's disgruntled employee with a Glock!

Right, more "Take care of your people, your posse and your pussy and they'll take care of you" Truth XXII again.

* * * * *

"Don't spend what you don't have, to buy what you don't need, to impress folk you don't even like."

----Tavis Smiley, 2011

LXXXIX.

In for a sip, in for a sea.

In 49 BC, fresh from his victories conquering the "barbarians" to the north of Italy, Roman general Julius Caesar was sent strict orders from the Roman Senate (who ruled Rome at the time) that he was not allowed to bring his army any closer to the city of Rome than the Rubicom River far north of the city.

The Senators were all afraid (and rightly so it turned out) that the always popular and now powerful Caesar would enter Rome and seize power.

DefYing the Senate, Caesar crossed the Rubicom and became

Rome's first Emperor. Since then, the phrase" crossing the Rubicom" has\meant making a choice you can't tum back from.

A hundred and fifty years before Julius Caesar crossed *his* Rubicom, Hannibal faced an almost identical decision from which there was no turning back.

At the end of the I'' Punic War, victorious Rome told defeated Carthage that none of Carthage's army was allowed to go any further north into Europe than the Ebro River (on the border of what is now northern Spain).

To go any further than that would start the war back up.

Hannibal deliberately went a lot further than that: not only crossing the Ebro but then crossing the "impassable" Alps to catch the Romans by surprise in their own backyard!

From the minute he first dipped his foot in the Ebro, Hannibal knew there would be no turning back.

When Nat Turner first looked towards Massa's house with hatred in his eye and a sharp machete in his hand, there was no turning back.

When Rosa Parks first refused to give up her seat on the bus, there was no turning back.

When Malcolm X broke with Elijah Muhammad, the die is cast and there was no turning back.

Despite threats to his life, the Reverend Dr. Martin Luther King Jr. knew there was no turning back.

On the flip side, prisons are packed with plenty of people who probably wish they would have turned back, while they still had a chance.

And, for all we know, half the people lying in the graveyard might be thinking the same thing!

Never let the arbitrary orders of others, or your fear of failing keep you from "crossing the Rubicon", of making a life-changing decision and *commitment* to *improve-conquer! --yourself* and our surroundings:

> "Most people can't help the way they are or don't care to change the things in themselves that need improving, but it's up to me not to allow a situation to develop that would hurt me."
>
> ----Evander Holyfield[145]

*   *   *   *   *

"Making a commitment" requires:

(1) *Acting with the best of intentions.* What you're planning will benefit yourself, others, and your environment.

(2) *Knowing what you're doing.* This means realistically having the skills to accomplish the mission and accepting the responsibilities involved.

(3) *Acting on good information* (after having double-checked your sources).

When we know our information's well and that our cause is just, some would say we then have a *responsibility* to act, to commit ourselves to proper action.

What's that old saying that "You gotta stand for something, or you'll fall for anything."?

---

[145] *Becoming Holyfield: A Fighter's Journey by* Evander Holyfield with Lee Gruenfeld. Atria Books/NY 2008.

"Commitment powers dreams and goals into reality...
with commitment you can change not only your life but
the world around you...You are fully committed to your
goals when you decide that nothing will throw you off
course in your pursuit of them. Not racism. Not threats
of violence. Not despair or disparaging words of other
people. When you commit to your goals, you develop
the attitude that no one can stop you."

---Isaiah Thomas, 2001

Of course, life isn't a soup-kitchen. Everything comes with a price:
"Those who are not afraid to commit themselves to the things they
believe in often wear scars, both seen and unseen. They wear them
proudly because those scars remind them of the battles they've fought
and won-even those that they've lost but not let defeat them." (Ibid.)

*　*　*　*　*

"It doesn't matter if you can win as long as you give
everything in your heart."

---Michael Jordan

XC.

**Mercenaries at least fight for pay...Fanatics fight for
anything...and for nothing!**

Rome always had a big professional army of "Legionnaires", so
naturally they criticized Carthage for hiring "mercenaries", men who
got paid for fighting.

But, if you really think about it, *everybody gets paid,* or at least they should.

"Altruism" (all-true-ism) is when you do something for someone-like a kindness-for nothing, when you help someone "out of the bottom of your heart", without having any desire to get "paid".

Altruism is a myth.

Everybody gets paid

One guy demands to be paid-Franklins up front! --for anything he does.

And people *should* be paid for their work.

Another guy takes the time to stop and help you get your car out of the ditch but then refuses your offer to pay him for helping you, because he believes he's supposed to be a "Good Samaritan"[146] and that The Lord will bless him later with a reward in Heaven.

One guy's getting paid in the here-and-now, the other guy's getting paid in the hereafter.

But, one way or another, *everybody gets paid*

The secret to getting what you want is getting people to do what you want, and you do that simply by (1) telling them what's in it for them, "making it worth their while", and (2) making sure they actually get paid (so they'll be more willing to help you again).

The way to do this is by learning to "read" the other person's personality, to figure out whether they're the kind who needs paid in cold hard cash or with God's warm embrace?

---

[146] From the Bible, Luke 10:37.

Sorry, you can't live up in the hills like some Smoke Jensen mountain man, or like that anti-social Unabomber nut (who still had to come down out of the hills every now and then just to blow people up!).

We have to live with people so we have to learn to *deal* with people.

Of course, some people you can talk to, some you can't[147]

For example, it's a lot harder bargaining with a fanatic wearing a suicide-vest since the "payday" he's after is a stack of dead *bodies* not a stack of dead presidents!

In Truth XCIII, when Hannibal warns us that "Too much lights blinds as surely as too little", he's talking about fanatics.

There's nothing wrong with being a "fan"--even if it does come from the word 'fanatic"! --just so long as every now and then you take the time to show excitement over something a little more "important" in life than your favorite team making a touchdown.

Then there's the others who take it to the opposite extreme. They *pretend not* to care about anything, "playing it cool", preventing themselves from showing any interest or excitement about *anything* because they're *afraid* if they show too much obvious interest in anything (or anybody) some sinister hater will find a way to use that interest to "control" them.

Relationships 101: This explains why some men have so much trouble with their personal relationships: they *fear* and *resent* the "control" their lovers have over them, paranoid that their lover will mistake their desire/need for love and companionship for weakness...and use that "weakness" to manipulate them.

This fear and resentment are reflected in the crude, politically-incorrect and sexiest joke that "Men love *pussy*...they just hate the package it comes in!"

---

[147] See "The Six Rules of *No-qotiation*" in Iung & Prowant's Ultimate Mind Control (Citadel Press,2011)

Bottom line: There's nothing wrong with your getting rewarded---paid, one way or another---for your sincere effort and hard work... because Life is sure going to *punish* you if you choose to go in the other direction!

There's nothing wrong with showing your excitement about something *positive*, about being dedicated and *committed* to a worthwhile cause:

> "That's why if you want to be extreme about something, be extreme about loving. Or be extreme about giving for a living. Be extreme about following your vision. Be extreme about surrounding yourself with positive people. Be extreme about practicing good Karma. Be extreme about counting your blessings. Be extreme about starting today. Be extreme about empowering yourself. Be extreme about spitting truth to power. These are the principles you should always try to be passionate about. Not shutting people out, or putting them down, or harming them because they seem to be different."
>
> ---Russell Simmons, 2007

XCI.

Victors sing the victory songs. Dirges to the defeated. Which sounds sweetest of all to The Gods?

War cries!

Everybody loves a winner. We love to party with entrepreneurs, entertainers, and end zone dancers just hoping some of their "magic" will rub off on us.

But don't crow if you can't throw.

And the only thing worse than a sore loser is a sore winner.

Don't brag when you win. And don't cry crocodile tears when you lose.

Far Eastern schools of philosophy like the *Taoists* in China and *Zen* in Japan practice arts of self-control like concentration, meditation, and martial arts so that when things go bad and the shit hits the fan, they won't panic.

But they also study these disciplines so they won't get too *excited-distracted*-- when everything just seems to fall into place and everything's going their way, so they won't get too full of themselves, not pay attention to details, and mess up.

The ancient Greeks had a group called *Stoics* who taught that a person shouldn't get too excited when things were going right, because things can go wrong at any minute.

On the flip side, no matter how shitty a hand you've been dealt, there's still a chance you can walk away with that Texas Hold 'em pot.

Come hard or don't come at all.

Even the God of The Bible warns that, if you're "lukewarm" you'll be spit out[148].

Nut up or shut up.

Take another look at Truth LXXXIX's comments of commitment.

* * * * *

---

[148] Revelation 7:16.

"Hope is a great falsifier of truth. What's real, is what's realized. Dig the mind game. We sacrifice our dreams for the illusion of security."

---Mtume, *Theme for Theatre of the Mind*

XCII.

No true gift comes with tax, toil, or tail attached.

In the classic 1967 movie *Cool Hand Luke* Paul Newman plays a smart-mouthed convict doing time in a southern prison where he keeps getting beaten down by guards while the Warden tells him:

"We're only doing this *for your own good,* boy."

Body bruised and beaten but spirit unbroken, Luke finally looks up and snickers,

"Wish you'd stop being so *good* to me, Boss!"

If you're going to do someone "a favor"...do them a *real* favor, no strings attached. And don't come back later throwing it up in their face, trying to obligate them into doing something for you.

Don't get "duty" and "obligation" confused:

- *Duty is* the debt you owe yourself to do the right thing because you promised--signed up-to do the right and people are depending on you to keep your word.

- *Obligation* is what people try to convince you you owe them for some real or imagined favor they've done you in the past.

233

Sometimes the best favor you can do someone is *not* to do them any favors.

Right, back to the Truth XC where we learned to tell people up front what's in it for them.

Part of telling people "what's in it for them" is telling them straight up how much doing something (or not doing something) is going to *cost* them.

Nobody likes hidden fees and strings attached:

- A puppy makes a cute Christmas gift…until you have to buy a new carpet by New Years.

- A smoking' hot woman doesn't stay smoking' hot for long, not if she turns out to be "high-maintenance".

- That new "over-stocked" flatscreen you bought cheap out of the back of that van parked in the alley is "Da bomb!".... that is until you're reminded- the hard way-that there's still a law in this state against "receiving stolen merchandise"!

Nobody likes "a deal" when there's hidden fees, strings, or *hand cuffs* attached.

XCIII.

No shadow walks without some light.

No light that doesn't carry its dark brother.

So, with shadows, so with men.

Too much light blinds as surely as too little.

The light of truth never casts a false shadow.

Another follow up to Truth XC.

Just as everyone has their "price", so too *everything comes with a price.*

You have to pay to play. Nobody rides for free.

It's no "conspiracy". There's nothing "sinister" about his universal fact. It's just the cost of *adults* doing business together.

In the military they call this "logistics": making sure you have enough men and material to move to the right place at the right time... usually, in *a hurry!*

When you're running a *business-before* you're running a business-you have to consider how much is it going to cost you to:

- *Get in the game.* (aka "ante up", your projected cost for start-up):

- *Stay in the game* (by anticipating your "overhead", the day-to-day cost of operating); and

- *Get ahead in the game.* (aka "cost assessment", what's working and what's *not* working for your individual projects, products, and purchases.). In other words, deciding what you keep and what-and *who-you* have to kick to the curb.

Who to kick to the curb?

Words and phrases like "desperate", "no other choice" and "too late" are not your friend and neither is any person-no matter how close they are to you-who keeps pouring that kind of poison in your ear[149]

No matter how bad things might look, you always have at least *two* ways to go: forward or back.

Standing still is *not* an option.

Stop making your choices in life based on prejudices or on personal preference, paranoia, or on problems you've encountered in of the past.

Rank your choices in order of *possibilities,* with each doorway you courageously step through suddenly revealing *two* more doorways for you to choose from. These two new doorways, in turn, each showing you two more, for a total of four new possibilities.

Four become eight, eight become sixteen, and so *on...endless possibilities!*

And, yes, sometimes *both* your initial choices are going to suck.

So, when forced to choose between "the lesser of two evils"...always choose the one that's *harder.*

That way, even if you fail, people will be impressed that you didn't take "the easy way" out.

Read Truth LXXXII again...take a deep breath...and then make your decision.

*   *   *   *   *

---

[149] Another reference to Shakespeare's *Hamlet.*

XCIV.

To be thankful for what you have been given, remember what was given up.

Slavery isn't something that only happened "back in the day".

Quiet as it's kept, slavery still goes on in many parts of the world. And, if you were born before October 2"d, 1979, then there were still slaves-at least one slave---still alive in the United States during *your* lifetime. That's the day Charles Smith, born a slave, died in Florida at the age of 137 years old.[150]

The road is long for some, all too short for others. But all of us are called upon to Make sacrifices along the way.

"Discipline" is measured by what we can do without and "sacrifice" is measured by what we're called upon to endure, what we suffer and yet ' keep on going---what Shakespeare's Hamlet called "the slings and arrows of outrageous fortune".

To get where you are today, you gave up something

- To hit "The Big Time" you gave up club-hopping' and hit the books instead. You give up a night on the town so that someday you might *own* that town!

- Or maybe you just gave up "chasin' tail" because you finally found the love of your life and didn't want to screw it up... *again.*

- Maybe you decided to get clean and stay sober but had to "sacrifice" Being "popular" with all your "meth-head friends".

---

[150] Anderson, 1997:19.

- Maybe you risked getting put on your boss' shit-list at work by speaking up for safer working conditions for you and your co-workers?

- *Maybe 5-0 now has you "in their sights" because you wouldn't* take the stand and tell lies on your innocent friend.

All the stories of all the great heroes and holy men down through history have one thing in common: *Their sacrifices.*

Sure, we praise the lessons they taught and the actions they did, but we should remember first and foremost. all they first had to give up---and had to endure-in order to learn what they learned in order to do all they did.

Others before us have "been there, done that".

Some have even "been there, done that...and gotten *killed* for doing "that", for even being "there".

So when you're standing there complaining about all you're going to have to give up to get where you want to be, take a minute to remember all those who came before you who gave up so much-some even giving up their lives-defending your right to, and demanding you be given an equal opportunity to, *complain.*

If you learn nothing else from studying the sacrifices made by those who've come before you-from heroes and holy men, to civil rights leaders, to members of your own family-it's this:

It's not about what you give up, it's about *not giving up.*

WHY DIDN'T SOMEBODY TELL ME'?

Though everybody remembers the 1989 movie Denzel Washington[151]

---

[151] Denzel won the Best Supporting Acting Oscar for his role.

and Morgan Freeman movie *Glory,* about the heroic all-Black 54th Massachusetts Regiment formed in 1863, the first Black man to actually serve in the Union Army during the Civil War was. James Stone, who did so 2 years earlier in 1861, fighting with the First Fight Artillery of Ohio.

Stone was killed while fighting in 1862.

XCV.

No spire higher than fire, no ocean deeper than fate.

———————————————

Nimrod (aka Orion) was a mighty hunter who became the world's first king[152] founding the empire of Shinar where he began building the "Tower of Babel", a great pyramid from which he could study the stars (a tower "reaching to Heaven", get it?)

God destroyed Nimrod's tower, not because God was afraid it would actually "reach to Heaven" but because Nimrod had gotten a little too big for his britches[153] and had forgotten who signed his paycheck!

The ancient Greeks had a similar story about a boy named Icarus who in order to escape his island prison made himself a man-size pair of wings out of feathers and wax which, unfortunately for the late Icarus, *melted* when he flew too close to the sun.

Both these stories are telling us the same thing: you can never build your ivory tower too tall, or fly too high-get too famous, too rich, too powerful-that you can't still fall flat on your face.

O.J.; Peewee Herman; Iron Mike; Amy Winehouse; Ray Carruth; Lindsey Lohan; Jerry Sandusky; Michael Vick....the list is endless.

---

[152] See the Bible book of Genesis chapters 10-11.
[153] Todays fancy words "arrogance" and "hubris". Look them up!

Don't be so stupid or so starved for attention, or both, that you end up adding *your* name to the list.

But...if your name does end up on TMZ in such dubious company:

(1) Congratulations! You made the big time.

(2) Nine times down, *ten times up!*

THE TRUTH ABOUT DEATH & LOVE

XCVI.

My son will die today. My son will die a hundred years hence. My tears will taste the same. Grief does not take notice of the sun's passing.

———————

"Your children are not your children. They are the sons and daughters of life's longing for itself. They come through you but not from you, and though they are with you, yet they belong not to you."

----*The Prophet* by Kahlil Gibran (1883-1931)

This was the poem Tupac Shakur's mother Afeni---former Black Panther, former drug addict, now right with God-read to her comatose son as he lay on his deathbed[154]

✳   ✳   ✳   ✳   ✳

---

[154] See *the Last Days of Dead Celebrities* by Mitchell Fink (Hyperion/NY 2006:149)

Remember Truth I? About doing something stupid that makes us lose the things you love the most?

If we really thought first about endangering, hurting, and losing the things---and *the people-we* love the most, would we still do half the stupid shit we do?

> Would we continue to put ourselves-and the people we care about---in harms way.

> "In peace, children bury their parents; war violates the order of Nature and causes parents to bury their children."

> ----Herodotus, Greek philosopher 485-425 BC

* * * * *

WHY DIDN'T SOMEBODY TELL ME?

The modern English word *"thug"* comes from the ancient East Indian word *"Thuggee"* (pronounced "tug-gee"), a killer cult, supposedly destroyed in 1837, who strangled people to please their *Black-faced* Goddess Kali[155]

The word "mugger" was a slang term also used to describe the Thuggee, since "mugger" (originally pronounced "mucker"). meant a crocodile that would stay hidden in the muck (mud) until striking its victim...like a *thug!*

XCVII.

Death is death no matter from what direction she comes to embrace you.

---

[155] See *the Ancient Art of Strangulation by* Dr. Haha Lung. Paladin Press,1995

We can't choose what happens to us in life, only how we *respond* to it.

There's a big difference between a "reaction" and a "response".

A "reaction" is something you do *without thinking.*

Babies are born with some reactions already (like jumping when they hear a loud noise). The fancy term for this natural *survival instinct* is "Flight or Fight", meaning we either run away from something because it scares us, or else we stay and try to beat the hell out of it!

A "response", on the other hand, is a *trained* reaction.

You think ahead to something that *might* happen and you make plans to deal with it if it does happen. For example: you anticipate that "So and so is going to say something (like they always do) and it's going to piss me off (like it always does!). But this time instead of going off on them (like I usually do), I'm going to play it cool and not give them the childish *reaction* they're looking for."

Or, how about when some big mouth tries to put his hands on you?

You're going to naturally *react* and either beat feet or else stand your ground and "defend" yourself, right? Its only common sense you'll have a better chance of giving Big Mouth some real work if you box regularly (if only to keep in shape) or if you spend some, time at the *dojo* perfecting your "Bruce Lee".

Reacting without taking the time to think things through is just your funeral waiting to happen.

But let's keep it real: Other times you have to move *fast* just to stay ahead of the game--just to stay *alive*! -and you got no time to "think" about what you *should* be doing.

That's where your *previous training* pays off.

Training yourself to better control your raw emotions (anger, fear, lust, and greed) prevents your enemies "yanking your chain" any time *they* choose.

Remember the original 1972 *The Godfather* movie? Sonny Corleone was a hot-head with what today we kindly call an "anger management problem" and his enemies used that *weakness* to play him like a sucker, to make him run off half-cocked...while they waited in ambush for him at the toll-booth[156] with *their* Tommy-guns fully cocked!

Likewise, how many men (thinking with "the little head" rather than "with the big head") have sniffed after some sweet piece of tail all the way to bankruptcy, prison bars or burial?

"Control your emotions or they'll control you" is a warning repeated over and over again down through history from wise men to warrior alike, from Aesop and Buddha to Sun Tzu and Hannibal.

In the same way we can't always control our reactions, most times we can't choose the way we die.

But we do have a lot of *choice* on how we *live* our lives between the womb and the tomb.

The Samurai warriors of Japan always lived every day of their lives as if it were their *last* day. They called this *Bushido*-"*The* Way of the Warrior"[157]

Rather than being depressing, knowing that Death kept their number on speed-dial made the Samurai *appreciate* life even more, making them treasure their friends and family even more (because you could lose them at any time).

As a result, the Samurai put up with a whole lot less *petty* bullshit!

*   *   *   *   *

---

[156] "at the *toll-booth,* get it? One way or another, *everybody pays* in the end.

[157] Check out Forest Whitaker's 1999 movie *Ghost Dog: Way of the Samurai.*

"I believe we come into this world through a revolving door: we leave and then we come back again. Call it reincarnation or whatever you want to call it...The key, I think, is to die on your own terms. If I can'tgofucking, I just want to go quietly, without interruption."

---Whoopi Goldberg, *Book, 1997*[158]

XCVIII.

Better an early death than a late trial.

———————————————

"The fame of one valiant in achievement shall not perish in this land forever."

------Ahmose, Admiral to the Egyptian
Pharaoh (1580-1501 BC)

* * * * *

"It is a good day to die!"

------Crazy Horse, at The Battle of the
Little Big Horn, 25 June, 1876

* * * * *

"My father, we must all die sooner or later, and if my time has come nothing will hold it back. It is far, far

---

[158] Rob Weisbach Books/William Morrow and Company, Inc./NY 1997:175

better to die with the joy of battle in the heart than pine away with age, or like a sllck ox in kraal. I have lived by the spear and I shall die by it. This is a man's death."

----Mgobozi Msane, General in the service
of ShakaZulu, October, 1826

*   *   *   *   *

"It is better to die on your feet than to live on your knees!"

------Emiliano Zapata,
1877-1918 Mexican Revolutionary

*   *   *   *   *

"But if it cost me my life in the morning, I will tell you tonight that the time has come for the black man to die fighting. If he's going to die, die fighting."

------Malcolm X

*   *   *   *   *

"Like anybody, I would like to live a long life. Longevity has its place. But I'm not concerned about that now. I just want to do God's will. And he's allowed me to go up to the mountain. And I've looked over, and I have seen the promise land. I may not get there with you, but I want you to know tonight that we as a people will get to the promise land...so I'm happy tonight. I'm not worried about anything. I'm not fearing any man."

--The Reverend Dr. Martin Luther King Jr.
April 3, 1968, the night before his assassination.

*   *   *   *   *

IC.

Love and death are the only things of value that come looking for us.

"There are too many people in the world, and not all of them useful. I know dead men who are more useful than half the living! I have learned so much more from the dead than I ever have from the living.

Death is the only thing of importance in a man's life.

All else is only preparation."

                                  ----*The Answers of Attila*

*   *   *   *   *

"Everything has an end."

                                  ---Masai proverb

Conclusion To Book

"But how can we ever hope to cross those mountains with 40,000 men, a long Baggage-train of supplies, and even great elephants in tow?" Hannibal's brothers Are said to have asked him, as they all stood staring up at the "impassable" Alps.

"We will find a way...else we will *make* a way!" Hannibal confidently declared.

And that's just what he did.

Here then is Hannibal's first *and final* lesson:

You say what you mean. You mean what you say.

- *You say what you mean.*

You make your intentions clear, first to yourself and then to others around you.

By doing this you give others fair warning to either help you ...or else get out of your way!

Here is the beginning of *respect.*

- *You mean what you say.*

You keep your word. You pay your bills. You do what you promised to do.

Consistency builds credibility.

Here is the beginning of *honor.*

With these two, Hannibal conquered his world.

And *you* can do the same.

Sources & Suggested Reading

- Ali, Muhammad, *The Greatest: My Own Story.*

- Anderson, Claude, Ed.D *Dirty Little Secrets: Secrets about Black History, it's Heroes, And other Troublemakers.*

- Babcock, Michael A., *The Night Attila Died.*

- Bernal, Martin, *Black Athena.* Rutger's University Press,.

- Brown, Tony, *Black Lies, White Lies: The Truth According to Tony Brown.* William Morrow and Company,.

- Cary, M. D.L.H. and H.H. Scullard, F.B.A., *A History of Rome,* 3rd ed. Macmillian,.

- Dungy, Tony with Nathan Whitaker, *Uncommon.* Tyndale,.

- Fink, Mitchell. *The Last /Jays of Dead Celebrities.* Hyperion!NY.

- oFlipper, Hemy. *Black Frontiersman: The Memoirs of Henry. Flipper.* Texas Christian University Press,.

- Gardner, Chris. *The Pursuit of Happyness.*

- Goldberg, Whoopi. *Book,* Rob Weisback Books/William Morrow & Company,.

- Goldworthy, Adrian. *Roman Warfare.* Smithsonian Books, 2005.

  --In the Name of Rome. A Phoenix Paperback/Wiedenfeld & Nicholson,2004 2nd Ed. 1993.

- Holyfield, Evander, *Becoming Holyfield: A Fighter's Journey.* Atria Books/NY.

- Lamb, Harold, *Hannibal: One Man against Rome*. Doubleday & Co., Inc.,.

- Lao Tzu, *Tao Te Ching*. China c. BC. (Mise, Translations).

- Lung, Dr. Haba., *Theatre of Hell: Dr. Lung's Complete Guide to Torture*. Loompanics Unlimited,.

  - Lung, Dr. Haba and Eric Tucker. *Nine Halls of Death*. Citadel Press/NY

  - Lung, Dr. Haba. *Mind Sword*. Citadel Press,.

  - *Assassin! Secrets of the Cult of the Assassins*. Citadel Press,.

  - *Lost Arts of War*. Citadel Press,.

  - *Absolute Mind Control*. Publication pending.

  - *Mind Dragon: The Lost Secrets of the Tao Warrior*. Publication pending

- Lung, Dr. Haha & Christopher B. Prowant, *Black Science*. Paladin Press, I

  - *Mind Manipulation: Ancient & Modern Ninja Techniques*. Citadel Press,.

  - -. *Mind Warrior: Strategies for Total Mental Domination*. Citadel Press.

- Machiavelli, Nicollo, The *Prince*.

- Malcolm X, *By Any Means Necessary*. Pathfinder.

- *Millennium Year by Year*. Edition,.

- Musashi, Miyamoto. *A Book of Five Rings (GoRin No Sho)*, Japan, (Misc. translations).

- Nietzsche, Friedrich. *Thus Spake Zarathustra.*

- Perrett, Bryan. *Last Stand! Famous Battles Against the Odds.* Cassell Military Paperbacks. London,.

- Potter, T.W., *Roman Italy.* University of California Press,.

- Rand, Ayn. *Anthem,.*

- Simmons, Gene, Me, Inco Dey **St.**

- Simmons, Russell. *Do You! Laws to Access the Power in YOU to Achieve Happiness and Success.* Gotham Books,.

- Sister Souljah. *No Disrespect.* First Vintage Books/ Random House,.

- Sobel, Brian with Jerry D. Morecock. *"Greatest Generals"* Armchair General magazine, March [159].

- Soren, David. *Carthage.* A Touchstone Book/ Simon & Schuster,.

- Spearman, Dr. Andre. *Baphomet: The Secret Power of Symbolism.* Hidden Agenda Publishing,.

- Sun Tzu, *The Art of War (Ping Fa).* China c. BC. Misc. Translations.

- Thomas, Isaiah. *The Fundamentals: Plays for Winning the Games of Business and Lift.* Harper Business,.

- Turner, Nat. *The Confessions of Nat Turner..*

- Waitley, Denis. *Seeds of Greatness,.*

- *Warriors,* Rubicon Publishing,.

---

[159] Declares Hannibal to be one of the greatest generals of the ancient era.

- Wells, PeterS. *The Battle that Stopped Rome.* W. W. Norton & Company, NY/London.

- Westheimer, Dr. Ruth, with Sr. Stephan Kaplan. *Power: The Ultimate Aphrodisiac.* Madison Books, I.

- Young, Fred J., *How to Get Rich and Stay Rich.* Lifetime Books, Inc.

- Smiley, Tavis, *Fail Up.* Smiley Books/ Hay House, Inc.

- DeBeer, Gavin Sir, *Hannibal: Challenging Romes' Supremacy.* A studio Book/The Viking Press/NY 1969

Printed in the United States
By Bookmasters